YORK NO

C000099807

MAKING HISTORY

BRIAN FRIEL

NOTES BY RACHEL HEWITT

Longman

York Press

The right of Rachel Hewitt to be identified as Author of this Work has been asserted by her in accordance with the Copyright, Designs and Patents Act 1988

YORK PRESS
322 Old Brompton Road, London SW5 9JH

PEARSON EDUCATION LIMITED
Edinburgh Gate, Harlow,
Essex CM20 2JE, United Kingdom
Associated companies, branches and representatives throughout the world

Quotations from *Making History* by Brian Friel are from the edition of the play published by Faber and Faber in 1989

First published 2006

10 9 8 7 6 5 4 3 2 1

ISBN—10: 1–405–83565–6
ISBN—13: 978–1–405–83565–7

Illustrated by Neil Gower
Phototypeset by utimestwo, Northamptonshire
Printed in China

CONTENTS

PART FOUR
CRITICAL HISTORY

PART FIVE
BACKGROUND

PART ONE

INTRODUCTION

HOW TO STUDY A PLAY

Studying on your own requires self-discipline and a carefully thought-out work plan in order to be effective.

- Drama is a special kind of writing (the technical term is 'genre') because it needs a performance in the theatre to arrive at a full interpretation of its meaning. Try to imagine that you are a member of the audience when reading the play. Think about how it could be presented on the stage, not just about the words on the page.

- Drama is always about conflict of some sort (which may be below the surface). Identify the conflicts in the play and you will be close to identifying the large ideas or themes which bind all the parts together.

- Make careful notes on themes, character, plot and any sub-plots of the play.

- Why do you like or dislike the characters in the play? How do your feelings towards them develop and change?

- Playwrights find non-realistic ways of allowing an audience to see into the minds and motives of their characters, for example, an aside or music. Consider how such dramatic devices are used in the play you are studying.

- Think of the playwright writing the play. Why were these particular arrangements of events, characters and speeches chosen?

- Cite exact sources for all quotations, whether from the text itself or from critical commentaries. Wherever possible find your own examples from the play to back up your opinions.

- Where appropriate, comment in detail on the language of the passage you have quoted.

- Always express your ideas in your own words.

These York Notes offer an introduction to *Making History* and cannot substitute for close reading of the text and the study of secondary sources.

 QUESTION

Conflict can be internal – in the individual's mind – and external – in wars. Which form of conflict is most important to *Making History*?

READING *MAKING HISTORY*

Making History grew out of Brian Friel's response to criticisms levelled at his 1980 play, *Translations*. *Translations* depicts the translation of Irish place names into English, under the authority of an Ordnance Survey map-making project in the early nineteenth century. The project is conducted by the English army, who later lay waste to the village of Baile Beag (Ballybeg), after a soldier's disappearance. The Ordnance Survey director, Captain Lancey, is portrayed as a crass, violent man. He represents certain English colonial attitudes towards Ireland. *Translations* was attacked by some critics regarding its historical inaccuracies. J. H. Andrews, a historian of the Ordnance Survey's activities in Ireland, pointed out that the real-life surveyors would not have carried bayonets, and would have had no part in the military control of the rural Irish population. In *The Achievement of Brian Friel*, 1992, the critic Sean Connolly added that the translation of place names was really carried out by Irish scholars, not the English military. Connolly concluded that Friel's account of the Ordnance Survey in *Translations* is 'a hostile caricature'. Friel openly admitted to his historical inaccuracies in the play. An admission of guilt was not enough, however. Friel felt bound to justify his distortion of historical fact. *Making History* grew out of his justifications of the playwright's right to manipulate historical 'truth'.

Making History can be read on two levels. It describes the reflections and relationships of the real-life historical figure of Hugh O'Neill, the Earl of Tyrone, before and after his failed rebellion against the English in **Renaissance** Ireland. In this way, Friel's play is about history itself. On another level, *Making History* examines how O'Neill's rebellion was represented by historians, and how O'Neill was turned into a hero for the Irish people. In this way, Friel's play is about how history is written. The word 'history' has a double meaning. It refers to the past, and to the written version of the past. It refers to events happening 'in history', and also to the 'histories' in which they are described. *Making History* explores how 'history' – in both its senses – is made.

> **CONTEXT**
>
> The Renaissance period, in which *Making History* is set, saw England become a unified state. England then began the task of moulding the world in its own image, using its new-found power as a nation.

In French, 'history' – or *histoire* – has another meaning: 'story'. This suggests that written histories may share characteristics with stories. Fiction, the need to tell a good story, may be more important than adherence to historical fact. Peter Lombard, O'Neill's historian, indicates this when he wonders 'isn't that what history is, a kind of story-telling?' (p. 8). In *Making History*, Friel considers whether the historian – and the playwright – should be faithful to the truth, or to the needs of a good narrative. This is expressed in terms of loyalty. Should the writer be loyal to history, to past events, and accurately represent all the facts and the evidence? Or should the writer remain loyal to the needs of history-writing, of *histoire*, and impose, as Lombard puts it, 'a pattern on events that were mostly casual and haphazard … shaping them into a narrative that is logical and interesting' (p. 8)? The themes of loyalty and betrayal are central to *Making History*.

Brian Friel has argued that drama and history-writing are fundamentally different. In his view, plays are not as obliged to fact and truth as histories. Replying to J. H. Andrews's criticisms of *Translations*, Friel argued that 'drama is first a fiction, with the authority of fiction. You don't go to *Macbeth* for history'. Friel's play *The Enemy Within* carries the disclaimer that it is 'neither a history nor a biography but an imaginative account, told in dramatic form'. In the programme notes for the original performance of *Making History,* Friel describes this **genre** in more detail. '*Making History* is a dramatic fiction that uses some actual and some imagined events in the life of Hugh O'Neill to make a story', Friel explains. He's mostly tried to 'be objective and faithful' to the known facts of O'Neill's life. Sometimes, though, tensions arose between the demands of fact and the demands of fiction. In those cases, Friel declared, 'I'm glad to say I kept faith with the narrative', with the need to tell a good story.

Friel's argument is more complex than the suggestion that drama and history are different disciplines with different loyalties. In *Making History*'s programme notes, he argues that *all* histories, however truthful in intent, end up as stories, fictionalisations of the facts. 'History and fiction are related and comparable', Friel says. Written histories attempt to locate an order and pattern in the historical evidence. Lombard describes how his history of O'Neill

 CHECK THE BOOK

Richard Pine, in *The Diviner: The Art of Brian Friel*, 1999, suggests that *Making History* considers the 'question of what a play *should* be faithful to, of what pieties it should observe'. 'Piety' derives from a word meaning 'duty', and is bound up with *Making History*'s exploration of the ideas of loyalty and betrayal.

 CHECK THE BOOK

In *The Nature of History*, 1970, Arthur Marwick quotes C. N. L. Brooke's description of the divided role of the historian: 'At the one extreme historians amass and analyse evidence, very much like a descriptive science … at the other extreme we analyse the play of human personality and all the subtleties of the human mind, and so mingle with literary criticism'.

will offer 'a cohesion to that random catalogue of deliberate achievement and sheer accident that constitutes your life' (p. 67). Written histories are selective of the facts. They select, order and interpret the evidence according to the need to create 'a narrative that people will read and be satisfied by' (p. 67). And so too, says Friel, does fiction.

In *Making History*, Lombard's fictionalisation of O'Neill's life is motivated by his desire to create a 'national hero' for Gaelic Ireland. His history will be a 'narrative that has the elements of myth' (p. 67). To create this myth, Lombard rewrites O'Neill's defeat against the English at the battle of Kinsale, which O'Neill describes as 'a disgrace' (p. 67). Lombard instead represents the battle as a 'legendary … triumph', 'the crushing of the most magnificent Gaelic army ever assembled' (p. 65). In history, the battle of Kinsale marked the beginning of the end of Hugh O'Neill's rebellion against the English in Ireland. Since Henry VIII's reign, England had accelerated its colonisation of Irish territory. *Making History* is set during Elizabeth I's reign, in which this colonisation became systematised. O'Neill attempted to unite the numerous Gaelic clans of Ireland under the shared aspiration to drive out the Protestant English. He sought the aid of another Catholic nation, Spain, who sent soldiers and arms to Ireland. O'Neill's rebellion came to a head at the battle of Kinsale. The Gaelic and Spanish forces were decisively defeated by the English. O'Neill was forced into hiding, and eventually left Ireland in 1607, along with other Gaelic chieftains, for the continent and exile. This departure was named 'The Flight of the Earls'. O'Neill's rebellion was a crucial moment of Irish resistance in the history of English colonisation. As Lombard describes, O'Neill has been an important mythic hero for Irish nationalists past and present. On the surface, *Making History* is about Renaissance Ireland, but the play is also a product of the era in which it was composed. In the late 1980s, tension between the nationalists and the unionists (who supported the union between England and Ireland) was intense. Tony Coult, in *About Friel: the Playwright and the Work*, 2003, points out that mythic heroes – such as hunger-strikers – were evoked in support of political arguments at this time.

CHECK THE FILM

The 1996 film *Michael Collins* offers a useful portrayal of the tensions between nationalists and loyalists in early twentieth-century Ireland.

CONTEXT

Here 'nationalism' in Ireland means opposition to a union with England.

The history play is a well-established genre. Some of Shakespeare's most famous history plays are the three concerning kings Henry IV and Henry V, which culminate in Henry V's defeat of the French at the battle of Agincourt. Friel has summed up the task of the traditional history play by referring to the words of Shakespeare's contemporary, Thomas Heywood: 'to teach the subjects obedience to their king; to show the people the untimely ends of such as have moved tumults, commotions and insurrections'. Friel's history play *Making History* does something quite different. In Heywood's view, a history play should celebrate the monarch and criticise the rebel. In Friel's version, it celebrates the rebel against the monarch. Friel's chief source for *Making History* was Sean O'Faolain's history of O'Neill, *The Great O'Neill*, 1942. O'Faolain explained that the traditional history play's formula is so accepted that 'we are liable to forget that there existed in the sixteenth century an alternative myth, that of the ancient Hero rising against the new Tyrant, or the local feudal knight against the king'. O'Neill's life provides the material for an alternative history play.

Making History was first performed by the Field Day Theatre Company at the Guildhall in Derry in Northern Ireland, in September 1988. After a run at the Guildhall, it toured twenty-one towns and cities. Amongst these locations was Tullyhogue Castle, at Dungannon, where the O'Neills' crowning-stone was held. Tullyhogue is mentioned in the first moments of *Making History*: O'Neill is invited to 'a big christening party' (p. 1) there. The actor Stephen Rea, who played Hugh O'Neill, described the experience: 'It's extraordinary to be somewhere you know that O'Neill definitely was … In Dungannon that night, it was the centre of everything, you know? Ten-year old[s] … were sitting knowing that their place was the centre of history, you know? It's great!' In the performance of *Making History* at Tullyhogue Castle, history (the facts) joined hand in hand with history (the fiction).

 CHECK THE BOOK

Sean O'Faolain was a novelist who decided to write a popular account of Hugh O'Neill. This was published in 1942 as *The Great O'Neill*, and was Brian Friel's starting-point for *Making History*. In his preface O'Faolain suggests that O'Neill's case would make good subject-matter for a play: 'a talented dramatist might write an informative, entertaining, ironical play on the theme of [O'Neill] helplessly watching his translation into a star in the face of all the facts that had reduced him to poverty, exile, and defeat'.

PART TWO

THE TEXT

NOTE ON THE TEXT

Brian Friel's Making History *was first performed by the Field Day Theatre Company at the Guildhall in Derry, on 20 September 1988. It went on to tour twenty-one towns and cities in Northern Ireland and the Republic of Ireland. The play was published by Faber and Faber in 1989. This remains the standard edition, and is used in these Notes. Any page references refer to this edition.* Making History *is also available in Brian Friel: Plays 2, Faber and Faber, 1999, with an introduction by Christopher Murray. An actor's edition was published by Samuel French in 1989.*

SYNOPSIS

CHECK THE BOOK
In her *Faber Critical Guide* to Brian Friel, 2000, Nesta Jones points out that one effect of placing the major events offstage is that 'Friel has a considerable amount of information to convey to the audience regarding both historical background and current events'.

Making History is a play in which almost nothing happens. Its historical context is the turn of the seventeenth century in Ireland, and the rebellion of the Gaelic chieftains, led by Hugh O'Neill, Earl of Tyrone, against the English. The turning point of O'Neill's rebellion, and the main event of *Making History*, was the battle of Kinsale in 1601. At Kinsale, the clans and their Spanish allies were routed by the English forces. *Making History* pivots around Kinsale. But, despite its central position between the play's two Acts, the battle is not seen onstage. The play consists of speculation, anticipation and planning before the event. After the event, there is analysis, lamentation and discussion concerning the battle's historical representation. In *Making History* action is replaced by discussion. Language and representation take precedence over historical event. This allows *Making History* to become a forum for debate regarding the relationship of history-writing to history itself.

Making History begins with Hugh O'Neill and his private secretary Harry Hoveden on stage. Their mutually dependent relationship is established right away: Harry is devoted to O'Neill, and O'Neill relies on Harry. Harry tries to inform O'Neill of his forthcoming responsibilities in his two public roles. O'Neill is a Gaelic chieftain responsible for County Tyrone's Irish inhabitants and an earl who has pledged allegiance to the English crown. The conflict between these two roles emerges through the play. At this early stage, O'Neill is buoyant and distracted, engaged in distributing flowers around his home. The reason for his distraction is explained: the night before, he married his third wife, Mabel Bagenal. Mabel is the daughter and sister of successive Queen's Marshals; she might be expected to reside firmly on the side of the Protestant English 'Upstarts' in Ireland. On the surface, Mabel is an odd choice of wife for a Catholic Gaelic chieftain.

The Catholic Archbishop Peter Lombard, and the young Gaelic 'prince' Hugh O'Donnell burst in on O'Neill and Harry. Lombard has just returned from a trip to the continent, where he visited the Pope, and the King of Spain. It emerges that the four men – Lombard, O'Donnell, O'Neill and Harry – are planning a decisive rebellion against the Protestant English in Ireland. As Catholics, they have sought the aid of the Pope and the Catholic King Philip II of Spain. Lombard has managed to secure a promise of aid from Spain, on the condition that the numerous Gaelic clans of Ireland cease warring and unite. Lombard is excited about the future, and about these four men's power to make – or change – history. He has decided to write a history of the rebellion, focusing on O'Neill's role. O'Neill is worried about Lombard's statement that, in his history, 'imagination will be as important as information' (p. 9).

When O'Neill tells Lombard and O'Donnell about his marriage to Mabel, they are horrified at the implications of his union with an English 'Upstart'. Mabel's entrance confounds the stereotype of an Upstart. She is an articulate and mature young woman, devoted to O'Neill. Their marriage represents the possibility of amicable Anglo-Irish cohabitation. At this stage, it appears possible.

Act I scene 2 takes place almost a year after scene 1, in 1592. It begins with a conversation between Mabel and her sister, Mary. Mary tries to persuade Mabel to leave O'Neill, but Mabel is adamant that his house is her 'home' (p. 24). The Anglo-Irish cohabitation appears to be enduring. A conversation between O'Neill and Mary, however, reveals that this domestic amicability is not replicated in the political sphere. There are tensions between the

> **CONTEXT**
>
> The tensions between the Irish and English are utterly bound up with religion. Whilst the Irish had a Catholic majority, the English were largely Protestant. During the Reformation, Catholicism was made illegal and fiercely punished.

English military and Gaelic clans. Preparations for O'Neill's rebellion are progressing. The Spanish finally promise military aid: soldiers, arms and a fleet of ships. The fleet plans to land in Kinsale, however, at the opposite end of the nation from O'Neill and O'Donnell's loyal tribes in the north. Their soldiers would have to march the length of the country to meet the Spanish, across a line of English fortifications. O'Neill is adamant that under no circumstances should the Spanish fleet land in Kinsale.

Between Acts I and II, eight months have passed. In that time the Spanish fleet landed in Ireland, at Kinsale; the Gaelic troops tried to meet up with the Spanish soldiers and consolidate their military strength; and the rebellion was defeated by the English. In Act II, O'Neill, O'Donnell and Harry are hiding out in the mountains, and Lombard has gone permanently to Rome. Ireland is in chaos: the English forces have exercised violent retribution against any of O'Neill's sympathisers, and the Irish population is starving. O'Neill has decided to write a formal submission to English authority, in exchange for the 'nominal' return of his title of Earl of Tyrone, 'without political or military power whatever' (p. 48). O'Donnell is shocked and saddened by O'Neill's submission to the English. Harry brings the devastating news that Mabel is dead, having died in childbirth along with her newborn baby.

Making History's final scene takes place in Rome 'many years later' (p. 54). O'Neill has remarried, and drinks heavily. He is staying with Lombard and Harry, and lives off a papal pension. Lombard has completed his history of the rebellion, and has represented O'Neill as 'a God-like prince' (p. 56), not a failure. Lombard explains that the Irish people need a 'hero' to believe in, and a 'heroic' literature to read, rather than the 'truth' (p. 67). O'Neill battles against Lombard's distortion of his identity. He pleads with Lombard to 'record the *whole* life', to 'put it *all* in' and show him as 'the schemer, the leader, the liar, the statesman, the lecher, the patriot, the drunk, the soured, bitter émigré' (p. 63). The play ends with two conflicting representations of O'Neill recited aloud, Lombard's celebratory history of O'Neill's Gaelic military prowess and O'Neill's grovelling submission to English political authority in Ireland.

CONTEXT

For Friel, language has the power to change, not just how history is represented, but how history is made. The users of language, the writers, poets, and playwrights, take on a political importance. 'I see no reason why Ireland should not be ruled by its poets and dramatists', Friel stated in *A Paler Shade of Green*, 1972.

DETAILED SUMMARIES

ACT I SCENE 1 [PP. 1–6]

- It is late August, 1591. O'Neill's personal secretary, Harry Hoveden, is informing O'Neill of his forthcoming duties as chieftain of County Tyrone.
- We get the impression that there is significant tension in the relationship between the English and the Irish inhabitants of County Tyrone, and internal tension within the Irish community.
- Harry informs O'Neill that the Archbishop Peter Lombard is writing a history of his life.
- We learn that O'Neill has recently married for the third time, to the sister of the English Queen's Marshal, Sir Henry Bagenal. Bagenal has been made angry by the mixing of English and Irish blood that is occasioned by this wedding, and he is likely to cause problems.

The play opens in the living room of Hugh O'Neill's home in Dungannon, County Tyrone. Whilst O'Neill is moving around, cutting and arranging flowers, his personal secretary Harry Hoveden tries to inform him of his various duties as the chieftain of County Tyrone. Harry is an efficient administrator, but O'Neill is not paying full attention, and appears more interested in the name of the flowers that he is distributing around the room.

Harry begins by listing O'Neill's commitments over three days in mid-September 1591. Among these is a christening party at Tullyhogue. Harry details more of O'Neill's responsibilities, and in particular describes a request from the English Lord Deputy that O'Neill's eldest son Hugh attends the newly founded Trinity College in Dublin. Harry informs O'Neill about forthcoming social engagements, and about problematic members of the Tyrone community, naming the O'Kanes, the Devlins and the Quinns in particular. O'Neill's concentration wanders throughout this list of responsibilities. He is brought abruptly to attention when Harry

> **CONTEXT**
>
> Trinity College was founded in Dublin in 1592. It promoted the teaching of the Protestant religion and endorsed the English language. Were O'Neill to send his son to Trinity College, it would seem to betray his Catholic, Gaelic-speaking roots.

CONTEXT

'Young Essex' is Robert Devereux (1566–1601), second Earl of Essex. He was appointed Lord Lieutenant of Ireland in April 1599, but displeased Elizabeth I. In 1601, he was executed in England for treason. His conferences with O'Neill in September 1601 directly led to his fall from favour.

CONTEXT

An Upstart is a newcomer in respect of rank and significance. The Gaelic chieftains often perceived the English colonisers as Upstarts who lacked their own ancient culture and nobility.

mentions that in England 'young Essex' (p. 4) has been arrested and imprisoned for treasonous conferences with O'Neill. In conclusion to his list of administrative tasks, Harry informs O'Neill that Hugh O'Donnell and Peter Lombard are waiting outside the door. O'Neill is taken aback and reluctant, and becomes wary when Harry explains that Lombard is writing a history of him.

Before O'Neill admits O'Donnell and Lombard into his living room, Harry hands him a letter, explaining that it is from Sir Henry Bagenal, the Queen's Marshal. Harry refers to O'Neill's recent, third, marriage to Mabel, who is Bagenal's younger sister. He warns O'Neill that Bagenal's letter expresses abusive anger at the mixing of English and Irish blood occasioned by the marriage. The text of this letter in *Making History* derives from Sean O'Faolain's biography of O'Neill, *The Great O'Neill*, 1942. O'Faolain described how Bagenal, upon hearing of Mabel and Hugh's marriage, 'swore to high Heaven in his rage to think that his "honest blood", that had so often been spilt in repressing this rebelly race, should be mingled with a pack of traitors like the O'Neills'. O'Neill becomes angry at Bagenal's letter, and dismisses him and his fellow Englishmen as mere 'Upstarts' (p. 6). O'Neill denies that Bagenal's letter requires immediate attention, and he makes to exit. He plans to convert a room that currently houses Spanish saddles into a bedroom for himself and Mabel.

COMMENTARY

The play begins with Harry's mention of 'a big christening party' (p. 1), a naming ceremony which indicates birth and new beginnings. This compares the coming-into-being of the play with the coming-into-being of a child. Both acquire a legitimate presence through the power of words, the child through its new name, the play through its words. In *Making History* a newborn child or heir represented the hope for a clan's power to last over another generation. O'Neill's hope for the lasting ascendancy of his clan is renewed by Mabel's pregnancy at the end of Act I scene 2. Hope is represented by a christening. The failure of that hope is marked by the death of the child. Harry informs O'Neill of the death of Mabel and her child when he has surrendered to the English in Act II. The death of a child means the death of hope.

The first dialogue of the play establishes the contrasting personalities of Harry and O'Neill. Harry communicates his authority in short simple statements of fact (**declaratives**). Contrastingly, O'Neill's speech comprises mainly questions (**interrogatives**). What is the effect of this? O'Neill's questions illustrate his mediation between opposing political factions – he listens to both sides of the story. Harry alludes to O'Neill's Irish and English acquaintances, and O'Neill's negotiation of his two roles as chieftain of the O'Neills, and an English earl. O'Neill's political adaptability is also illustrated by his two accents, his *'upper-class English accent'* (p. 1) and his *'Tyrone accent'* (p. 3). However, O'Neill's questions also indicate his irresolution, and his susceptibility to influence. Later in the play, this proves crucial to his rebellion's failure. O'Neill's indecision is also exhibited in his speech's disorderly nature. He flits from subject to subject and rarely pursues conversations initiated by Harry. When Harry attempts to focus O'Neill on the christening of Brian O'Hagan's first child, O'Neill instead asks the name of the flowers he is distributing around the room.

In *Making History*'s first few minutes, there are many references to historical figures, political events and geographical locations. Harry and O'Neill refer to Sir William Fitzwilliam, Sir Garret Moore, Sir Robert Gardener, 'young Essex', Sir Henry Bagenal, the O'Hagans, O'Kane, the Devlins and the Quinns. They discuss Brehon law and the founding of Trinity College, Dublin. Places such as Tullyhogue, Roosky in Roscommon, and Mellifont Abbey are also mentioned. Harry and O'Neill's dialogue conforms to **realism**. The characters do not explain these historical allusions. The historical Harry and O'Neill would have been extremely familiar with the references, which would have required no explanation. Friel's conversational realism may initially exclude members of the audience unfamiliar with Irish history and geography. However, the unexplained historical references of *Making History* may encourage the audience to fill in the play's gaps, to correct its distortions, and to become better acquainted with the history of the British Isles.

The geographical references in this section are particularly important (see **Geographical background**). The christening that opens the play takes place in Tullyhogue. Tullyhogue was the site of

CHECK THE BOOK

The New Historicist school of literary criticism relates apparently minor details in a text to their historical context. In his famous work of new historical criticism, *Shakespearean Negotiations*, 1987, Stephen Greenblatt begins with the premise that the presence of historical references in a text is never an 'accident'.

the pre-Christian inauguration stone of the O'Neills: it is the site of the christening of Hugh O'Neill, as well as of Brian O'Hagan's son. In fact, the O'Hagans were hereditary stewards to the O'Neills, and they lived at Tullyhogue Fort. In the play, Harry refers to this fact when he reminds O'Neill that Tullyhogue was 'where you were fostered' (p. 1). At this point of the play, Tullyhogue represents hope for the future: hope for the future of O'Hagan's son, hope that the past authority of the O'Neills will continue into another generation. However, historical knowledge hints that this hope is unfounded. In 1601, the English Lord Deputy of Ireland, Mountjoy, marked his victory against O'Neill by smashing the stone at Tullyhogue. O'Donnell will describe this in Act II (p. 46). The initially impenetrable historical references that punctuate this opening section of the play are clues that, with a little research, may reveal the end of the play and the failure of O'Neill's rebellion. *Making History* encourages a type of reading that is akin to detective work.

GLOSSARY

1	**Tullyhogue** a town in County Tyrone, almost due north of Dungannon, O'Neill's residence
1	**genista** the Latin name for the Spanish broom plant, which looks similar to a rush
1	**Virgil** a Roman poet (70–19 BC), renowned for his poem on the founding of Rome, *The Aeneid*
2	**Lord Deputy** a person appointed to exercise authority on behalf of the sovereign power, in this case in Ireland. Sir William Fitzwilliam acted as Lord Deputy of Ireland between 1572 and 1575
2	**the new Trinity College** a university founded by the English crown in Dublin in 1592. It promoted the Protestant religion over Catholicism, and the speaking of English over Gaelic
2	**Annual Festival of Harpers** the harp is an important component of traditional Gaelic music
2	**Roosky, Roscommon** a town in County Roscommon, situated to the west of the centre of Ireland
3	**Limavady** a town in the north of Londonderry, a northern Irish county

3	**tribute** the term for a tax, a rent payment, or a payment in homage by a subject to his leader
3	**gallowglass** a member of a particular class of soldiers maintained by Irish chiefs in this period, renowned for ruthless violence
3	**Mellifont Abbey** the residence of Sir Garret Moore, a firm friend of O'Neill, in County Louth. O'Neill stayed there in 1603 after the defeat of his rebellion, where he submitted his surrender to Elizabeth (without being informed that she had died a few days earlier). He was granted a pardon, known as the Treaty of Mellifont
3	**Lord Chancellor** the official secretary of the monarch, in charge of all letters, charters and official writings
3	**Lord Chief Justice** the term designated to the senior Irish judge responsible for the execution of law in Ireland, under English rule. Lord Chief Justices were active in Ireland from the early thirteenth century to the early twentieth century
4	**Brehon Law** the legal code that prevailed in Ireland before the English occupation. It was conducted through the arbitration of a Brehon, a professional judge, whose post was hereditary. The Brehon could decide the amount of the fine levelled on the guilty party, but left it to the family, chiefs and patrons of the injured party to obtain payment. Brehon law was abolished in the reign of James I
4	**the new English Law** English observers were critical of the Brehon's inability to enforce the punishment of the guilty party. They were also critical of the absence of capital punishment from Brehon law. When the Devlins threaten to seek retribution against the Quinns through the new English Law, it is because they predict it will more successfully exact a greater penalty
5	**Queen's Marshal** a high office of state, entrusted with the sovereign's military affairs
6	**Helen of Troy** the daughter of Zeus, reputed to be the world's most beautiful woman. Paris abducted Helen to Troy. The Trojan War began when the incensed Greek leaders attempted to win her back

CONTEXT

Mabel Bagenal came to be known as the 'Helen of Troy' of the Irish wars. Mabel's marriage to O'Neill exacerbated the anger of Henry Bagenal. O'Neill's comment that Mabel is 'not exactly Helen of Troy' (p. 6) is supposed to be a comment on her inferior beauty, but, in this historical context, is **ironic**.

ACT I SCENE 1 [PP. 6–12]

- Hugh O'Donnell and Archbishop Peter Lombard visit Hugh O'Neill.
- Peter Lombard has been in Rome, visiting the Pope. He has returned to Ireland via Spain, where he entered into discussions with the Spanish monarch Philip II regarding the possibility of Spanish support for an Irish rebellion against the English.
- Lombard relates these discussions to O'Donnell and O'Neill.
- O'Neill asks Lombard about the history he is writing. The two men discuss their different ideas of how a history should be constructed.

CONTEXT

The Anglo-Spanish war of 1585–1604 reached a climax in 1587 with Philip II's planned invasion of England by the Spanish Armada. The war continued for another seven years until a peace treaty was signed by Philip III of Spain and James I of England.

As Hugh O'Neill is about to leave to begin redecorating his bedroom, Hugh O'Donnell and Peter Lombard enter. Lombard gets straight down to business, and reports that he is carrying a letter from the Pope to O'Neill, regarding his request for support for his rebellion. O'Donnell is not paying full attention, however. Whilst Lombard speaks, he pours himself wine, and muses aloud regarding the rotting of floorboards at O'Neill's and his own mother's house.

O'Neill asks Lombard about the history he is writing. Lombard explains that there are two ways to write a history. On the one hand, the historian can pay attention to 'truth and falsity' (p. 8) and attempt to represent the facts accurately. On the other hand, factual accuracy can be put aside in favour of 'imagination' (p. 9) and the construction of a 'logical and interesting' (p. 8) narrative. Lombard defers a fuller explanation of his purpose as a historian until later in the play (see p. 66), commenting that 'history has to be made – before it's remade' (p. 9).

O'Neill's private secretary Harry Hoveden re-enters, and conversation turns to the English building of forts in strategic positions across Ireland. O'Donnell demonstrates how these forts will affect the Gaelic tribes' ability to support and communicate with one another. In particular, the north and the south of Ireland will be separated by a line of forts from Dundalk to Sligo, and a large fort at Derry will separate, and monitor any interaction between, O'Donnell and O'Neill (see **Geographical background**). This military separation of clans renders each one individually vulnerable. O'Donnell worries that the English will attack him and O'Neill once their counties of Donegal and Tyrone have been separated.

Lombard tries to reassure O'Donnell. He introduces his news from Rome and Spain, regarding support for an Irish Catholic rebellion against the Protestant English settlers. He reminds Hugh O'Neill of a letter he sent three months ago to Philip II of Spain requesting military and financial assistance. In return for help, O'Neill offered to restore the power of the Catholic Church. He would also grant Ireland as a kingdom to Philip II. Lombard explains that Spain is reluctant to help until the Gaelic tribes cease internal hostilities, and unite under a common ideal. Whilst Lombard recounts these discussions, O'Donnell tells of his own personal hostilities with the Gaelic chieftains O'Doherty in Inishowen and O'Rourke in West Breffny.

COMMENTARY

The different personalities of O'Donnell and Lombard are exhibited in their styles of greeting. O'Donnell is described in the stage directions as *'a very young man in his early twenties'* (p. 6). His informal manner is demonstrated by his affectionate embracing of O'Neill, his use of the colloquialisms 'man' and 'lads' (pp. 6–7), and his teasing of O'Neill about his new jacket (p. 6). In contrast, the initial exchange between Lombard and O'Neill is rather guarded, and Lombard makes a formal presentation of two gifts – a birdcage and a candelabra – from the Pope. Lombard is fluent in Latin, which indicates his formal classical education. O'Donnell cannot understand Lombard's Latin references (p. 12), which indicates that he's had a less formal education. O'Donnell is described as being *'impulsive, enthusiastic and generous'* (p. 6). His impulsive nature is illustrated by his difficulty in concentrating on the dialogue. This causes quick changes of subject matter, frequent interruptions and abrupt halts.

Hugh O'Donnell cannot concentrate on Lombard's news from Spain. While Lombard speaks, O'Donnell describes the rotting floorboards in O'Neill's house. This type of dialogue is similar to a

> **CONTEXT**
>
> The O'Doherty clan generally had good relations with the English, and were renowned for using this to cause arguments between O'Neill and O'Donnell. The clan did acquire a reputation for treachery, though. The Lord of Inishowen, Cahir O'Doherty (1587–1608), was made Admiral of Derry city by the English. Shortly after, he was provoked into burning the city, and was executed by the English crown. He became popularly known as 'that audacious traitor'.

CONTEXT

Ireland has often been represented in the image of a big house. The rotting of O'Neill's house is a **metaphor** for the problems that Ireland faces.

classical musical form, called 'counterpoint' or 'polyphony' ('many voices'). In counterpoint, one musical voice or melody is set against a different voice. They sound at exactly the same time, so that the ear hears both melodies at once. The form became popular in English music from the sixteenth century, and its relevance to Friel's writing is discussed in **Language and style**. O'Donnell's descriptions of rotting floorboards counterpoints Lombard's discussion of the news from Spain. They may sound different, but, in fact, the two voices harmonise. O'Donnell describes how his mother mended her own rotting floorboards with oak taken from the wrecks of the Spanish Armada. This alludes to an earlier Catholic resistance of the English Protestant Reformation, in which Philip II of Spain sent a fleet of ships in 1588 – the Armada – to attempt an invasion of England. After stopping in Calais, in France, the fleet was attacked by the English naval forces and had to retreat. By mending her floorboards with Armada oak, O'Donnell's mother constructs her house out of the failure of Catholic rebellion. O'Donnell's suggestion to Hugh O'Neill that he should 'do the same' (p. 8) hints at the coming failure of his own rebellion, and ties in with Lombard's explanation of Spain's caution regarding its support.

O'Neill and Lombard discuss 'the historian's function' (p. 8) and method. O'Neill uses words such as 'check', 'interpret', 'comment', 'truth', 'falsity' and 'accuracy' in his description of history-writing (p. 8). This indicates that O'Neill believes in a world of historical fact, an **empirical** reality, a single 'truth' (p. 8). He believes the historian's job to describe this reality is similar to the scientist's discovery of laws that define the universe. They both uncover the truth. Lombard, however, uses words like 'story-telling', 'narrative' and 'imagination' (p. 8) in his description of the historian's task. For Lombard, the world is too complicated to present a single 'right' history, and there are as many interpretations of the world as there are historians. He articulates this fully a little later in the play: 'I don't believe that a period of history … contains within it one "true" interpretation just waiting to be mined. But I do believe that it may contain within it several possible narratives' (p. 15). In Lombard's view, the historian's task is closer to the novelist's job, than to that of the scientist. The themes of history-writing and **historiography** are crucial to *Making History* (see **Themes** and **Historiographical background**).

When Harry Hoveden returns, the talk turns again to politics. O'Donnell describes the English plan to build fortifications across the country, to separate and diminish the combined strength of the Gaelic clans. O'Donnell illustrates this plan by pretending a sheet of paper is a map, and tearing it where the line of forts will be built. He rips the paper into quarters (p. 9). The use of a map as a theatrical prop is a powerful way of representing the large-scale politics of land in the small space of the theatre. A map is perhaps the archetypal theatrical prop. A map is also a visual symbol of national identity. When O'Donnell rips his 'map' into quarters, he illustrates the weakening of national strength and pride that will follow.

Lombard has received letters from the Spanish king and foreign minister. The texts of these letters are taken from one of Friel's historical sources: the introduction to Lughaidh O'Clery's *The Life of Hugh Roe O'Donnell*, 1603. Lombard emphasises that the unity of Gaelic tribes is fundamental to the success of O'Neill's rebellion. However, it becomes clear that this unity is prevented by more than the English fortifications. Lombard describes how Gaelic chieftains have been 'constantly at war' through history, 'always, always among themselves' (p. 11). He explains that the clans must join together to tackle the English. He points out that Spain will refuse to assist the rebellion until this co-operation is evident. O'Donnell counterpoints Lombard's hopes for Gaelic unity, with a description of his own arguments with nearby Gaelic chieftains.

CHECK THE BOOK

O'Donnell's quartering of the 'map' of Ireland alludes to the beginning of William Shakespeare's *King Lear*. This play begins with Lear showing on a map his decision to split his territory between his three daughters.

GLOSSARY

6	**Lough Owel** a lake situated 4 km north west of Mullingar, in County Westmeath. In 1597, the O'Neills burned down Mullingar
7	**my poor sister** O'Neill's wife prior to Mabel was O'Donnell's sister Siobhan
7	**Ballyshannon** the O'Donnells' castle was in Ballyshannon. In 1597, the English were defeated at the battle of Ballyshannon
7	**Commentarius** an abbreviation of the full name of Lombard's history, *De Regno Hiberniae, Sanctorum Insula, Commentarius*, meaning *Chronicler of the Kingdom of Ireland, the Island of the Saints*

8	**those Armada wrecks** the Spanish Armada was sent over towards Ireland in 1588, but the large Spanish fleet was defeated by smaller, nimbler English ships
9	**Counter-Reformation** the pan-European movement to combat the Reformation, which had forcefully asserted Protestantism over Catholicism
9	**Killybegs** a port in County Donegal, where a ship from the Spanish Armada stopped for repairs
10	**O'Rourke in West Breffny** the O'Rourkes took a leading role in the Nine Years War on the Gaelic side. Brian Na Murtha O'Rourke was hanged by the English for treason in 1591
10	**Lough Allen** a lake in County Leitrim, which would have been in the territory ruled by the O'Rourkes of West Breffny
11	**Duke of Lerma** when Philip II died in 1598, his son Philip III succeeded him. He was more intent on pleasure seeking, and left policy making to his ministers, in particular to the Duke of Lerma

ACT I SCENE 1 [PP. 12–19]

- Hugh O'Neill tells Lombard and O'Donnell that he got married the night before. They are taken aback.

- Lombard and O'Donnell are even more surprised when O'Neill reveals that his new wife is Mabel Bagenal, one of the New English, and sister of the Queen's Marshal.

- O'Neill introduces Mabel to Lombard and O'Donnell. All three characters find the introduction difficult.

O'Neill interrupts Lombard's history of Ireland with the announcement that, early that morning, he eloped to Dublin to get married. O'Donnell and Lombard are shocked, and O'Donnell tries to guess who O'Neill's new wife is. From the numerous possibilities, it's obvious that O'Neill is rather promiscuous. O'Neill describes his wife, Mabel. To O'Donnell and Lombard she appears unsuitable in every way. She is young, only twenty years old, one of the New English, Protestant, the daughter of the

CONTEXT

The position of Queen's Marshal was a high office of state, and was usually entrusted with the military affairs of the sovereign. In the summer of 1595, O'Neill carried out a successful attack on a large force under Sir Henry Bagenal, who escaped alive, but was seriously hurt. In *The Great O'Neill*, 1942, Sean O'Faolain describes Bagenal as 'the typical colonist, half-soldier, half-merchant ... [with] an implacable distrust of the native'.

previous Queen's Marshal, and the sister of the present Queen's Marshal. She appears to be, in every way, the enemy. O'Donnell labels her family 'half tramps' (p. 14).

While O'Neill exits to find Mabel, to introduce her to the men, O'Donnell describes in vivid detail the shocking violence perpetrated by Mabel's brother against the rural community of a nearby valley.

Mabel is introduced to O'Donnell and Lombard. She appears self-assured and innocently excited by her new situation. When O'Neill and Mabel are alone, she reveals how nervous she was. Their marriage suddenly seems very unequal: he is an older man, full of sexual and social self-confidence. She is rather out of her depth, and is overwhelmed by having rejected her family and background. Mabel seems resilient, however, and promises O'Neill that she'll be able to cope.

COMMENTARY

O'Donnell responds very noisily to O'Neill's announcement of his marriage. He exclaims, swears, and drums the table. He turns to and fro between O'Neill and Harry, expressing disbelief to both. He clearly considers Harry to hold some responsibility for O'Neill's actions. He perceives the two men as a unit. This perception is confirmed by Harry and O'Neill's own behaviour, as they take turns to answer O'Donnell's questions. O'Donnell's wild exclamations contrast with O'Neill's short statements at this point. The younger man appears impulsive and immature, but O'Neill is quiet and authoritative, in charge of the situation. His authority is reinforced when he gives a full explanation of Mabel's identity, in a formally-structured paragraph that contrasts with O'Donnell's half-finished sentences and colloquial speech.

O'Donnell describes the New English – and Mabel – as 'half tramps' (p. 14). A tramp is an itinerant person, someone homeless and continually on the move. Referring to a woman, the word hints at her sexual promiscuity. Mabel refers to O'Neill's mistresses as 'tramps' (p. 41). A sense of homelessness, of transient identity, pervades all Irish experience in *Making History*.

CHECK THE BOOK

In *Brian Friel and Ireland's Drama*, 1990, Richard Pine points out that tramps recur so often in Irish literature 'because the outsider, the deviant, the wanderer, the rebel, are central, rather than peripheral, to the way in which Irish society … exercises itself'. The tramp is a stock character in Irish drama. Samuel Beckett's play, *Waiting for Godot*, 1955, features two tramps and Friel's plays, *Crystal and Fox* and *Faith Healer* also feature travelling tradesmen who live out of suitcases rather than a house.

CONTEXT

Post-colonial literature explores the after-effects of colonial history. Inhabitants of countries that have been colonised often possess feelings of homelessness and exile, feeling that they live somewhere between the colonising and colonised cultures, but not fully in either one. In *The Satanic Verses*, 1988, Salman Rushdie describes 'the exile' as 'a ball hurled high into the air. He hangs there, frozen in time … denied motion, suspended impossibly above his native earth'.

A language can provide a type of home. O'Neill speaks two languages, English and Gaelic. He speaks in two accents, in the accent of County Tyrone and, as Mabel describes, 'like those Old English nobs in Dublin' (p. 17). Which accent does O'Neill feel most at home with? He speaks in a Tyrone accent when he is asserting his Gaelic identity, that Ireland 'is *my* country' (p. 14), and when he is expressing strong feelings. O'Neill speaks in *'an upper-class English accent'* (p. 1) in his public role, and when he wants to keep his feelings under control. O'Neill's interchange of the two accents could indicate a sense of homelessness, a displacement from both Gaelic and English cultures. Displaced characters in Salman Rushdie's novel *The Ground Beneath Her Feet*, 2000, similarly flit between languages and accents, and 'a sentence could begin in one language, swoop through a second and even a third and swing back round to the first'.

A marriage is an act of union. Marriage can be a **microcosm** for a political union. O'Neill's marriage to Mabel is a microcosm of a union between Ireland and England. As such, O'Donnell sees it as a betrayal of Irish interests, an acquiescence to English tyranny. He refers to their marriage as 'a class of treachery' (p. 14). O'Neill's marriage was also perceived as a betrayal of Catholic interests, to Protestantism. The bishop who married O'Neill and Mabel, 'Tom Jones, the Protestant Bishop' (p. 13), advocated extreme measures in the promotion of Protestantism in Ireland. O'Neill's two accents demonstrate his refusal to commit to either culture, and his 'treachery' of both. Historians have accused O'Neill of two-facedness or Janus-facedness, after the Roman God (see **Historical background**). The themes of treachery and duty run through *Making History* (see **Themes**).

O'Neill's marriage to Mabel will have dramatic political consequences. Violence is hinted at by Friel's use of butchery metaphors. Hugh O'Donnell refers to Mabel's brother, Henry Bagenal, the Queen's Marshal, as 'Butcher Bagenal' (p. 14). He compares Bagenal's killing of families in Finn Valley to the ruthless slaughter of animals. The English are not the only butchers, though. Mabel describes O'Donnell as 'Butcher O'Donnell' (p. 17). This complicates our view of the reprehensibility of the New English. Evidently, both the English and the Gaelic sides have a history of violence. The English poet and courtier Sir Philip Sidney used images of butchery in his attack on Irish barbarism, *A View of the State of Ireland*, 1633. Sidney suggested that the Irish turned into wolves once a year, drank the blood of living animals, painted themselves in battle with the blood of their friends and enemies, and drank the blood of executed prisoners. Brian Friel is tapping into the images of butchery that pervaded historical English and Irish descriptions of each other's violence. O'Neill also uses butchery and cannibalism **metaphors** when describing his lust for Mabel. He wants 'to devour' her (p. 17). This hints that O'Neill's marriage to Mabel is itself a form of Anglo-Irish violence.

O'Neill gives Mabel a watch, fitted on to a ring. He calls the watch a 'time-piece' (p. 19): it will allow Mabel to watch time pass, to watch the present becoming the past, to watch history being made. That the English queen Elizabeth I also possesses a watch indicates the privileged nature of this position. Elizabeth I and Mabel will clearly have different interpretations of O'Neill's history. We are reminded of Lombard's argument that history is more complicated than a single interpretation, but 'that it may contain within it several possible narratives' (p. 15).

CONTEXT

Clocks were first miniaturised into portable watches during the period in which *Making History* is set. The *Oxford English Dictionary* suggests that Shakespeare made the first reference to a watch in 1588 in *Love's Labour's Lost*.

GLOSSARY

12	**Brian McSwiney's daughter – the Fanad Whippet** the Fanad Peninsula was ruled over by the MacSweeneys. Rathmullan, where the Flight of the Earls started, is on the Fanad Peninsula. It is also where Hugh O'Donnell was kidnapped
13	**Siobhan Magennis** the name is a contraction of two of O'Neill's other wives
13	**New English** the settlers who were sent over to Ireland as part of the English policy of plantation of the north east of the country
13	**The Bishop of Meath … Tom Jones, the Protestant Bishop** was a fervent and violent anti-Catholic, who attempted to persuade Elizabeth against a policy of toleration of Catholics
15	**Tyrconnell** the Gaelic for 'Land of the O'Donnells'
15	**Titular Bishop of Armagh and Primate of All Ireland** from Latin, 'primus', meaning first – the title held by the Archbishop of Armagh. Lombard was made Archbishop of Armagh in 1601, whilst living in Rome

ACT I SCENE 2 [PP. 19–29]

- It is now 1592. Mabel has spent almost a year with Hugh O'Neill, and the changed furnishings of their house illustrate her influence.
- Mabel receives a visit from her sister, Mary. Mary tells Mabel about the changes to their lands at Newry. As a parting gift, Mary offers Mabel seeds.
- Mary is seriously considering a marriage proposal from the sixty-five-year-old 'young Patrick Barnewall' (p. 23).
- Mary is trying to persuade Mabel to leave O'Neill and return to Newry with her, when O'Neill enters. He tries to draw Mary into discussion regarding a dispute between Henry Bagenal and the Gaelic lord, Maguire. O'Neill describes his choice regarding which side to support.

Mabel initially appears more at home in her new territory. She has altered the room according to her taste. However, offstage shrieks in Irish from a young girl and boy terrify her, and it is clear Mabel is on edge. Mabel's sister, Mary, has been to visit her, and is preparing to go back to the family home at Newry. Hinting at her loneliness, Mabel tries to persuade her to stay, but Mary refuses. She gives Mabel presents from the estate at Newry – nectarines, quinces, honey and seeds – and describes the plantation of the surrounding land at Newry.

Mabel and Mary's father has recently died, and Mary describes his alert psychological state directly preceding his death. Mary is lonely too in Ireland, and is considering a marriage proposal from the sixty-five-year-old Patrick Barnewall. Mabel tries to persuade her to reject him, commenting that 'the man's an old fool … He has been a joke to us all our years!' (p. 23). This turns into an argument between the two sisters regarding the Irish people. Mary considers that 'they are not civilized' (p. 24), and Mabel retorts that 'as for civility, I believe that there is a mode of life here that is at least as honourable and as cultivated as the life I've left behind' (p. 24). Mary criticises what she sees as O'Neill's 'treacherous' (p. 24) nature, in his dual allegiance to the English Protestant crown and the Irish Catholic population of County Tyrone.

O'Neill and Harry enter. There are stilted civilities between Mary and O'Neill, and a warmer meeting of Mary and Harry. O'Neill questions Mary about her brother, Henry Bagenal, and his reaction to the threat posed by 'Maguire down in Fermanagh' (p. 26). O'Neill describes his own difficulty in assessing which party to support. Maguire is an old ally, and represents O'Neill's Gaelic heritage. Bagenal, and the English forces, represent a different form of civilisation which O'Neill 'grudgingly respects' (p. 28), and which have also played a role in his upbringing – O'Neill describes nine years of his childhood spent in England, amongst the aristocracy. Mary advises O'Neill to maintain allegiance to the crown, and leaves.

COMMENTARY

Mabel's terror at the shrieks of Irish youngsters playing around outside her house makes her angry. She shouts at them to 'shut up!' (p. 20). The youngsters cannot understand English, and Mabel's cries at them in English suggest that she cannot speak Gaelic. There is a communication breakdown. Mabel attempts to control the Irish by silencing them. Mabel accuses the young Irish couple of behaving 'like savages' (p. 20). Accusations of Irish 'backwardness' dominated English writing of this period. The English poet Sir Philip Sidney accused the Irish of 'barbarous rudeness' in his book *A View of the State of Ireland*, 1633. In *A New History of Ireland*, 1976, Moody, Martin and Byrne explain that English and Irish societies were constructed very differently. The English were unable to perceive the validity of Irish social structures, and so dismissed them as 'uncivilised'. **Metaphors** of savagery occur throughout this scene, and Mary refers to the rural Irish population as 'not civilised', steeped in 'superstition', and 'savage' (p. 24).

Mary describes the distance from Mabel, in Dungannon, to her house in Newry as 'a long way'. Mabel argues that 'it's only fifty miles' (p. 20). Mary and Mabel experience the distance of fifty miles very differently. Mary feels that Newry and Dungannon are very far apart: she uses distance to express the political and emotional difference between the Bagenals and the O'Neills. Mabel argues that

> **CONTEXT**
>
> The families of Hugh Maguire, O'Donnell and O'Neill were inter-related. Assisted by O'Donnell, and encouraged by O'Neill, Maguire launched a military campaign against English troops in 1593. Henry Bagenal overpowered the Maguires of Fermanagh, and seized Enniskillen Castle, a strategic position in his long-standing attempts to intimidate O'Neill. Two years later, however, in October 1595, Maguire regained Enniskillen Castle, again assisted by O'Donnell and O'Neill.

CHECK THE BOOK

Friel's play *Translations* examines the relationship between language and power. The English army official, Captain Lancey, denigrates the Gaelic language spoken by the Irish rural community. Lancey uses military and verbal power to dominate the play's Irish characters.

CONTEXT

The English appropriation and plantation of Irish land occurred systematically from the mid-sixteenth century. The English considered that the Irish were misusing the land through unproductive agriculture.

Newry and Dungannon are not so far apart: she wants to keep her family and home close, whilst remaining married to O'Neill. Scientific language may seek to represent a single truth, but there is no single interpretation of the human experience of distance. **Objective** truth is replaced by **subjective** feeling.

Mary uses grammar to illustrate her sense of the difference between her family and the O'Neills. She refers to the inhabitants of Dungannon in the third person plural pronoun, 'they': 'They have no bees here, have they?' (p. 20). This creates a 'them and us' relationship. Mabel expresses her allegiance to Dungannon, by referring to herself and O'Neill in the first person plural pronoun, 'we': 'No, we haven't' (p. 20). She allies herself with the O'Neills. Similarly, Mary uses 'home' to refer to Mabel's place within Bagenal's estate at Newry. Mabel redefines her 'home' as Dungannon (p. 24).

Mary describes the Bagenals' replanting of the land surrounding the estate. They have drained, ploughed and fenced a piece of bog land, and planted English fruit trees upon it. The Bagenals have confiscated Irish land; although bog land was considered useless by the English, it did possess significance. The geological matter that constituted Irish bogs was considered particularly interesting amongst scientific circles. In the nineteenth century, the directors of the Ordnance Survey in Ireland compared Irish bogs to a version of history in which nothing is forgotten: bogs are 'the accumulated result of ages'. Irish bogs represent the type of history-writing that O'Neill wants Lombard to employ, in which 'the *whole* life' (p. 63) is recorded. Bogs possess symbolic value in the Irish consciousness and the English appropriation of bog land denies this value. The planting of English fruit trees on the appropriated land enacts the section of Virgil's *Georgic* poetry that Friel refers to at the beginning of *Making History* (see **Extended Commentaries**, Text 1 – Act I scene 1 (pp. 1–4)). In Virgil's poetry, the broom represents native flora. The broom can be threatened by new plants, which may 'stifle its growth, dry up its fruitfulness' (*Georgics*, Book II). Here, English plants are doing just that. There is a more detailed discussion of Friel's use of gardening and plantation metaphors in **Themes**.

Mary and Mabel discuss the farming on O'Neill's land. Mabel describes it as 'pastoral farming – not husbandry' (p. 21). Pastoral farming involved using land as pasture for cattle or sheep, and Mabel describes the 'two hundred thousand head of cattle here at the moment' (p. 21). Pastoral farming characterised the Irish landscape, but was opposed by the English practice of arable farming. Arable farming, or 'husbandry' (p. 21), involved the ploughing and tillage of land ready for crops. The English settlers in Ireland considered that arable farming rendered the land productive, whereas pastoral farming was wasteful. Uncultivated land was, in the English view, a sign of an uncivilised society. For them, this legitimised the English appropriation and plantation of that land. Mary articulates this view. Pastoral farming, she says, is 'no farming – what you really mean is neglect of the land. And a savage people who refuse to cultivate the land God gave us have no right to that land' (p. 24). Mabel, however, can perceive the worth of pastoral farming, and she argues that the English and Irish are civilised and savage in equal measures.

The names of the seeds that Mary gives Mabel are significant. She would have given Mabel 'tansy, too, but I'm afraid it died on me' (p. 21). This is **ironic**. The name 'tansy' derives from a Greek word meaning 'immortality'. An apparently immortal herb has died on the Newry plantation. This could illustrate the Irish soil's rejection of English arable farming practices. Mary also warns Mabel not to let the fennel and dill cross-fertilise. Here, herbs are used as a metaphor for the cross-fertilisation of the English and Irish cultures. The result is, Mary suggests, 'a seed that's neither one thing or the other' (p. 22) – a hybrid. This is a version of the **post-colonial** argument that a colonised culture becomes a hybrid of its former nature and the colonising culture. Mary's image also alludes to a seventeenth-century poem by Andrew Marvell, 'The Mower Against Gardens', 1681. In Marvell's poem, exotic flowers are planted in an English garden. They all cross-fertilise in 'forbidden mixtures' and hybrids result: 'no plant now knew the stock from which it came'. Marvell uses plant imagery to encourage the 'purity' of English culture in England. In the same way, Mary uses herb imagery to encourage the separation of English and Irish cultures in Ireland. She feels so separate from the Irish that she doesn't even consider them to be people. When Mary's brother suggests that she should 'meet more people', she replies that 'we're surrounded by

CONTEXT

Mabel's estimate of the number of cattle on O'Neill's land is not excessive. During the Renaissance period, cattle were a key Irish commodity. Dairy products provided a dietary staple, and cattle were used for their hides and for beef. The main profit came from live cows exported mostly to west and south-west England. The Irish cattle trade was so strong that, in 1621, English and Welsh cattle producers sought laws to restrain the competition.

CONTEXT

Mary remembers when she and Mabel used to make tansy pudding at Easter. This was a traditional practice. The bitterness of tansy was thought to represent the bitterness of the Passover.

the Irish' (pp. 22–3). Mary doesn't consider the Irish to be people worth meeting.

When Mary tells Mabel about Patrick Barnewall's marriage proposal, Mabel responds that 'the man's an old fool' (p. 23). Mabel is gradually adopting her local dialect. Hugh O'Donnell had responded to O'Neill's account of his marriage to Mabel with the exclamation to 'quit the aul fooling' (p. 13). Now Mabel responds to Mary's account of her marriage proposal using exactly the same words. This language change indicates her sympathy with O'Neill and O'Donnell. Mary recognises this, and points out that Mabel is 'beginning to talk like them, to think like them!' (p. 25). O'Neill and Barnewall are both referred to as 'old fools'. The foolery O'Neill and Barnewall share is that of belonging to two opposing sides. The idea of 'foolery' is another aspect of the accusations of treachery that are levelled at O'Neill throughout the play. These accusations are explored in **Themes**, and the idea of foolery recurs in the next section.

O'Neill's greeting of Mary is tense, and is marked by a succession of very short questions and answers. His discussion with Mary regarding his decision whether to support Maguire or Bagenal's forces is similarly hostile. Both characters' speeches are marked by prepositions and possessive pronouns that appear to express unity between the English and Irish, but really illustrate their mutual opposition. O'Neill refers to the English encouragement of the Gaelic lords to 'come in' and articulate loyalty to the crown (p. 26). As O'Neill explains, the preposition establishes difference between those who are 'in' and those who are 'out'. The English sympathisers are 'in', and the resistant Gaelic lords are 'out'. Both O'Neill and Mary use the possessive pronoun 'our' to indicate supposedly mutual affection: O'Neill refers to 'our friend Maguire' (p. 28) and Mary refers to 'Our Henry' (p. 27). This is ironic, as no such mutual affection, no mutual possession or belonging, exists. Maguire is not Mary's friend, and Henry Bagenal is not O'Neill's. O'Neill's mocking repetition of the phrase 'Our Henry' illustrates this irony (p. 27). English grammar is used in this passage as a form of failed propaganda. It seeks to establish and reflect Anglo-Irish unity where none exists. O'Neill sees that the English and Irish are really 'two deeply opposed civilizations' (p. 28).

CONTEXT

In O'Neill's words, the New English culture is constituted of 'calculation, good order, common sense, the cold pragmatism of the Renaissance mind' (p. 28). The Renaissance period in England was defined by a revival of classical traditions in art and philosophy, which pervaded every aspect of society.

GLOSSARY

24	**The Cistercian monks in Newry** Newry was the historical site of a monastery and a Cistercian Abbey. After the dissolution of the monasteries in Henry VIII's reign, the Bagenals colonised the area
25	**Lucifer – the Great Devil – Beelzebub** synonyms for the devil
28	**The Book of Ruth** a book in the Bible, coming just after the Book of Judges
29	**valerian** herb with medicinal properties

ACT I SCENE 2 [PP. 29–37]

- Harry is in the middle of asking O'Neill about his intentions regarding Maguire, when O'Donnell enters, breathless with excitement.

- Lombard follows, and the two men convey their news. The Spanish have agreed to provide money, soldiers and arms to aid O'Neill's Catholic Irish Rebellion against the English. The Pope is also in support of the plan.

- O'Neill has a momentary pause, when he thinks back to his childhood spent amongst the English aristocracy. He quickly returns from his reverie to begin making plans.

After Mary and Mabel leave the stage, Harry questions O'Neill about his intentions regarding Maguire's request for support against Henry Bagenal. O'Neill, unexpectedly, after his celebration of Maguire's Gaelic heritage in the last scene, criticises his planned uprising. The outcome of such an uprising, O'Neill argues, is inevitable. The English forces are too strong, and they will defeat Maguire with violent consequences for everybody. However, upon Harry's gentle admonishment, O'Neill acknowledges that Maguire has no choice but to defend his Gaelic heritage.

O'Donnell bursts in, followed shortly afterwards by Lombard. They are both equally excited. They have heard news from Spain that the foreign minister and the king are prepared to support the rebellion that O'Neill has been planning. A fleet of Spanish ships is

CONTEXT

Fitzmaurice, McDermott, Nugent, O'Reilly, O'Connor and O'Kelly (p. 30) were the names of powerful Gaelic clans, all of whom attempted uprisings against the English and were defeated.

being assembled, with six thousand Spanish and Italian soldiers. Harry remains pragmatic throughout O'Donnell's excited chatter, and is worried that six thousand soldiers won't be enough to defeat the English. He is also concerned that the Spanish fleet will attempt to land on the opposite side of Ireland from County Tyrone, at Kinsale. O'Donnell is too overwhelmed by excitement to take Harry's concerns seriously. Lombard describes the Pope's support for the rebellion. The Pope has offered a Bull of Indulgence, which bestows forgiveness on any Catholic who takes part in the uprising. This redefines O'Neill's rebellion as 'a holy crusade' (p. 33) of Catholicism against Protestantism, rather than a political statement of Gaelic culture against English colonisation. For the Pope, the rebellion is less about Ireland specifically, than about global Catholicism. Peter Lombard is quoting from the genuine historical document that justified O'Neill's rebellion against the English, Pope Clement VIII's *Bull of Indulgence*. The *Bull* begins with exactly the same words as Friel's version: 'To the archbishops, bishops, prelates, chiefs, earls, barons and people of Ireland'.

O'Neill remains silent while receiving this news. He has a momentary reverie in which he remembers his childhood spent with the Sidneys at their Shropshire estate in England. In what is essentially a **soliloquy**, O'Neill describes his final evening at Sir Henry Sidney's castle, when Sir Henry drunkenly suggested that O'Neill would always be an outsider within English society. The Irish, he stated, only adopt English 'civilised' ways when they are compelled to do so. Left to their own devices, they are 'wild' (p. 35), and O'Neill is no different. Sir Henry's statement of distrust for O'Neill has eaten away at him since then. Now, however, O'Neill suddenly feels no anger.

O'Neill snaps out of his reverie, and begins making plans. He instructs Lombard to write to Spain, telling them under no circumstances to land at Kinsale. He wants the Pope's Bull of Indulgence to be increased to a Bull of Excommunication. This would excommunicate any Catholic who refused to actively support O'Neill's rebellion, and is more radical than the offer of forgiveness to Catholics who fight. O'Donnell informs O'Neill of a rumour circulating in Dublin that he's been proclaimed a traitor to the English, and that there is a substantial reward for his arrest. O'Neill considers this to be good publicity for his cause.

COMMENTARY

O'Neill's double-sided political allegiance is exhibited in the double-sided aspect of his speech characteristics. He speaks both in the accents of County Tyrone and unaccented English, and, in this scene, he intermittently *'roars'* and speaks *'softly'* (p. 30). The loudness and the Tyrone accent occur at acutely emotional moments, when O'Neill exhibits the impulsiveness, the 'capricious genius' and 'brilliant improvisation' (p. 28) that he defines as peculiarly Gaelic characteristics. O'Neill's quieter English voice is used at moments of greater self-control, when his thoughts are articulated in logical order and with less emotion. In these speeches, O'Neill demonstrates the 'good order, common sense, the cold pragmatism of the Renaissance mind' (p. 28). Both aspects – the Gaelic and the English – are equally present within O'Neill's personality.

In his discussion with Harry, O'Neill refers to Maguire as 'a fool' (p. 30). The word is repeated three times in this section, before O'Neill acknowledges that, in fact, 'Maguire's no fool' (p. 30). The word 'fool' has appeared before in *Making History*. Upon hearing of O'Neill's marriage to Mabel, O'Donnell told him to 'quit the aul fooling' (p. 13). Similarly, upon hearing of Sir Patrick Barnewall's proposal to Mary, Mabel described Patrick as 'an old fool' (p. 23). O'Neill and Barnewall, in these accusations, are both fools. They both possess a dual allegiance that pulls them in different directions. O'Neill is allied to the Gaelic clans of County Tyrone over whom he rules, and also to the English crown that allowed him his power. The historical figure of Barnewall was allied to his English aristocratic heritage, but also to the Catholic Church. If foolery goes hand in hand with a dual allegiance, then O'Neill's conclusion that Maguire is no fool is correct. Maguire is exclusively allied to what O'Neill describes as 'the composition of his blood' (p. 30), his Gaelic heritage.

O'Donnell bursts on to the stage, full of the excitement of news from Spain. His words are chosen for effect, rather than the imparting of information. His speech is repetitious – the word 'news' (p. 30) is repeated eight times, the word 'great' twice in one sentence (p. 31). O'Donnell's excitement is so great that the

CONTEXT

The fool was a stock character in Renaissance drama. Shakespeare's fools, in *King Lear* and *Twelfth Night* especially, are complex. They hang back from the action. They pass from character to character. They watch chaos unfold onstage, but offer comment at a distance. In the fool's refusal to ally himself exclusively to a single party, there are similarities with O'Neill's and Barnewall's 'foolish' behaviour.

CHECK THE BOOK

Casimir, in Friel's play *Aristocrats*, 1979, also talks more than the situation, or reality, requires. Language can make up for disappointment, it can substitute reality. In *Translations*, 1980, Hugh explains that excessive talk is essentially Irish, symptomatic of the national sense of disappointment. He says that Gaelic 'is a rich language ... full of the mythologies of fantasy and hope and self-deception – a syntax opulent with tomorrows. It is our response to mud cabins and a diet of potatoes'.

eloquence and **syntax** of his speech is disrupted. On two occasions, O'Donnell's descriptions increase in magnitude, from 'big' to 'huge' to 'enormous' news (p. 30), and from 'three' to 'four' people (p. 31). This is designed to increase the audience's feeling of suspense regarding the nature of his news. The suspense is increased further by O'Donnell's deferral of the revelation until Lombard is onstage. However, there is an element of insubstantiality to O'Donnell's excitement. He offers no information, only effect. He offers words, not substance. This is indicated by the emphasis he places on other speakers' words, rather than their meaning. He draws attention to the 'great word ... "pontificate"' (p. 33) and to the 'word flagship' which is 'like music to me!' (p. 36). However, O'Donnell does not look beyond the word to the meaning and detail. O'Donnell talks too much, more than his message requires. He talks so much that we are led to question his faith, our faith, in what he says. This inner insubstantiality of O'Donnell's speech could hint at the imminent failure of O'Neill's rebellion, and O'Neill is right to recognise that 'O'Donnell's enthusiasm worries me' (p. 39).

Peter Lombard's speech characteristics are different. His excitement is equal to O'Donnell's, but more under control, and his greeting of O'Neill and Harry is conventional and formal. Where O'Donnell repeats the same word, Lombard offers a series of **synonyms** – 'begging, cajoling, arguing' (p. 31). The effect is the same, however, and in Lombard's speech, as in O'Donnell's, the quantity of words employed exceeds what is necessary. The talk of both men is intended to impress, rather than to impart information. Lombard's recitation of the Duke of Lerma's full name, 'Don Francisco Gómez de Sandoval y Rojas, Fifth Marquis of Denia, Duke of Lerma, my friend, Ireland's friend' (p. 31), and the full title of 'His Holiness Pope Clement VIII' (p. 33) is an example. The recitation of rank is intended to inspire awe in his audience, and rally enthusiasm and faith in the success of the rebellion.

If Harry and O'Neill form one double act, Lombard and O'Donnell form another. The language of the two men is perfectly matched in this section. O'Donnell acts as a prompt for Lombard to speak, a type of compère who introduces and whips up enthusiasm for the following act. O'Donnell introduces, supports, sums up, applauds and seeks applause for Lombard.

O'Neill proves a disappointing audience. He remains silent. Harry simply seeks information regarding the details of the Spanish offer of aid. Harry and O'Neill's caution causes Lombard and O'Donnell's theatrical drumming-up of enthusiasm to fall flat. In **rhetorical** terminology, the descent from the elevated to the commonplace is called **bathos**. O'Neill, when finally provoked into response, drifts into a dreamy **monologue** regarding the nature of his allegiance to the English. The emotional foundation of his sympathy towards the English originated in the childhood he spent with the Sidneys. O'Neill's **soliloquy** is discussed in more depth in **Extended commentaries**, Text 2 – Act I scene 2 (pp. 34–5).

When he comes out of his reverie, O'Neill's language becomes efficient. He perceives the extent of the work to be done in preparation for the rebellion, and takes responsibility for it. In this, O'Neill differs from Lombard, who seeks to abdicate practical responsibility by dividing up and delegating work to be done. Lombard is reluctant to allow detail to deflate his enthusiasm. He dismisses aspects of the plan he regards to be 'a military matter' (p. 32) or 'a spiritual matter' (p. 37). O'Neill instead tends to see what Mabel will term 'the overall thing' (p. 39), the big picture. However, as the final section of this act will show, O'Neill admits that 'the overall thing – we don't even begin to know what it means' (p. 39).

GLOSSARY		
31	**The Council of State**	consultative branch of the Spanish government, whose recommendations are non-binding
32	**The Barraco in the province of Avila**	El Barraco is a region in central Spain. It was the birthplace of the Spanish general Don Juan del Aguila
33	**Dark Rosie**	an English translation of a Gaelic song – 'Roisin Dubh' – said to have originated in Hugh O'Donnell's camps. It is one of Ireland's most famous political songs. Roisin Dubh is a woman who represents Ireland, and looks forward to Spanish-Catholic aid against England, and inevitable defeat
33	**Holy Communion**	Christian ritual whereby a member of the church congregation receives wine and wafers as a representation of the blood and body of Christ
33	**Pontificate**	the reign of the pontiff, the Pope

continued

 CHECK THE NET

For the words of the song, 'Roisin Dubh', and an English translation, go to **www.irishpage. com** and click on 'Irish Song', and then 'Roisin Dubh'.

34	Frobisher and his officers Martin Frobisher (1535–94) was one of the most important explorers of the Renaissance period. In 1588 he was knighted for his role in the defeat of the Spanish Armada
35	Archbishop Oviedo a Spanish Franciscan who was made Archbishop of Dublin in 1600. He eventually found the Catholic-Protestant tensions in Ireland overwhelming, and in 1611 he returned to Spain

ACT I SCENE 2 [PP. 37–42]

- Mabel tries to persuade O'Neill not to go ahead with the planned rebellion, and he explains why he feels he must.
- Mabel tells O'Neill she's pregnant, and commands him to tell his mistresses to leave. He refuses.
- O'Donnell informs Mabel and O'Neill that a Spanish fleet is preparing to sail to Ireland, carrying military support for the rebellion. The fleet plans to land in Kinsale.

CONTEXT

In the same way that English monarchs had official mistresses, it was not unusual for Gaelic chieftains to do the same. One of the characters in Thomas Kilroy's play about O'Neill's rebellion, *The O'Neill*, 1962, is O'Neill's mistress, Roisin.

Mabel demonstrates that she has a clear and impartial understanding of the political motivations behind O'Neill's rebellion, and tries to persuade him to abandon the idea. She praises O'Neill's ability to mediate between the Gaelic and the English as the archetypal 'political method' (p. 38), and argues that taking the Gaelic side exclusively will almost certainly risk defeat. Mabel points out that England will throw every military resource into fighting an uprising, as Queen Elizabeth's only other choice would be to renounce control of Ireland. According to Mabel, Gaelic resources are insufficient to defeat English military power alone. The Spanish, however, do not have the same investment in winning the war as either the Gaelic or the English, and are consequently unreliable allies. Mabel also informs O'Neill that Charles Blount, Lord Mountjoy, is about to be appointed as Lord Deputy of Ireland, exercising power in the name of Queen Elizabeth. Mountjoy has a 'ruthless' (p. 39) reputation, and is to be feared.

O'Neill explains the difficulty of his task of preserving Gaelic heritage, whilst also seeking to modernise Irish society and allow it to reap what benefits English culture may introduce. He is critical of the colonial motivation behind England's presence in Ireland, and this provokes tension between O'Neill and Mabel. She demands that he ask his mistresses to leave, and he refuses. Mabel tells O'Neill she's pregnant, and he shows little interest. His subsequent apology is interrupted by O'Donnell, bringing news that a Spanish fleet is about to set sail, and it will land in Kinsale.

COMMENTARY

As Mabel tries to persuade O'Neill to abandon the idea of a Spanish-supported uprising, she speaks calmly and firmly, in declaratives. O'Neill, on the other hand, speaks in interrogatives. This bestows power and knowledge on to Mabel. This is similar to the opening scene of the play, in which Harry's authority was illustrated in his use of statements in answer to O'Neill's questions. Mabel also places great emphasis on the second person singular pronoun 'you' (pp. 37–8). Up until now the rebellion has been talked about in the name of Spain, and in the name of Catholicism and the Pope. Mabel refers to this as 'talking in code' (p. 39), in which Ireland merely becomes a symbol for something else. O'Neill's leadership has also been lost amongst Lombard and O'Donnell's enthusiasm for the support of the Pope, King Philip of Spain and the Duke of Lerma. Now, by emphasising the word 'you', Mabel focuses attention back on to Ireland's own importance, and on O'Neill as the leader of the uprising. She tells him that 'my only real concern is you, Hugh' (p. 39). She argues that, seen in this way, the war's result will not be in the favour of O'Neill or Ireland.

Mabel's use of 'you' rather than 'us' also distances herself from the plan. O'Neill employs the second person plural pronoun 'us' – 'This time Spain is with *us*' (p. 38) – to try and implicate her, but Mabel firmly extricates herself, reminding him that 'Spain is using *you*' (p. 38, my emphasis). O'Neill recognises this, and, by comparing Mabel to Queen Elizabeth (p. 38) and referring to her as an 'Upstart' (p. 39), suggests that they are on opposing sides in this war. When apologising, O'Neill adopts Mabel's language, and begins using the first person singular pronoun 'I' as an illustration of his acceptance of responsibility for a leading role in the rebellion.

CHECK THE BOOK

In his *Course in General Linguistics*, 1959, the linguist Ferdinand de Saussure suggested that a word was made up of two elements. The **signifier** was the letters or symbols of the word itself, and the **signified** was the meaning or idea it represented. The two together formed the **sign**. When Mabel refers to Lombard's use of Ireland as a 'code' for Roman power, she means that the signifier 'Ireland' has become separated from the signified, the reality of life in Ireland. It has merely become a word used in arguments whose interest lies elsewhere.

Despite O'Neill's apology, the precedent has been set for the disintegration of O'Neill and Mabel's relationship. Their ensuing conversation reflects this. There is a mutual lack of comprehension. O'Neill says that he can't 'even begin to know what' Mabel's argument 'means' (p. 39), and, when O'Neill refuses to dismiss his mistresses from the house, she asks 'what does sorry mean?' (p. 41). They no longer understand one another, and O'Neill's adoption of his Tyrone accent at this point reinforces the communication gap between them.

Mabel's statement that she is pregnant seeks to re-establish harmony between the couple. As the detailed commentary for the first scene of the play explains, a baby is often introduced by Friel as a representation of hope for the future. O'Neill's dismissal of the importance of Mabel's pregnancy dashes these hopes. His sarcastic use of the phrase 'if all goes well' (p. 41) in reference to Mabel's giving birth is **ironic** in the light of the fact that she, and the baby, will die in childbirth.

During O'Donnell's account of the consolidation of Spanish aid, he imitates a Spanish accent. In the play's text, his pronunciation is written phonetically: '"Beeg fleet – beeg ships"!' (p. 41). O'Donnell's attention to the superficial aspect of language, to its sound, suggests that he isn't paying full attention to its content, its meaning. This is reinforced when O'Donnell dismisses the importance of 'wherever Kinsale is' (p. 42). He merely enjoys the Spanish pronunciation of Kinsale as 'Keen-sall' (p. 42). As Harry has previously hinted, and as O'Neill's exclamation of 'Oh, God, no' (p. 42) indicates, the location of Kinsale is, in fact, of crucial importance to the success or failure of O'Neill's rebellion.

CONTEXT

The death of the mother, and often the child, in childbirth was a much more common event during the Renaissance than it is today. It was an affliction with no respect for class: Henry VIII's third wife, Jane Seymour, died whilst giving birth to Edward VI in 1537.

GLOSSARY

39	**Lord Mountjoy … Charles Blount** replaced the Earl of Essex as the queen's commander in Ireland. In 1600 he became Lord Deputy. After defeating O'Neill's rebellion, he was ruthlessly violent in his imposition of English rule across Ulster

ACT II SCENE 1 [PP. 43–8]

- Eight months have passed since the previous scene. O'Neill's rebellion has taken place, and the Gaelic and Spanish forces have been defeated at the Battle of Kinsale.
- O'Neill and O'Donnell are hiding out in the Sperrin mountains. Mabel is about to give birth, and has been taken to a safe house.
- O'Donnell relates his news regarding the state of the country, in the wake of the attempted rebellion. The news is not good. O'Donnell has resigned his role as chieftain, and is planning to leave the country.

In the dramatic time since the previous scene, O'Neill's rebellion has been defeated. He and O'Donnell are hiding in the Sperrin mountains. They have lost their possessions and are running low on food and water. English troops under Mountjoy cover the countryside, behaving with utter brutality towards the Catholic Irish. The nation is ravaged by famine, and, one by one, Gaelic lords and chieftains are surrendering to the English. O'Donnell suggests tentatively that their defeat at the battle of Kinsale was due to having been betrayed. O'Neill dismisses this notion.

O'Donnell tells O'Neill that he's resigned his position as chieftain of the O'Donnells and Tyrconnell, acknowledging that he was too impetuous: 'the blood gets up too easy' (p. 47). He is planning to go into exile on the continent, and leaves the next Friday.

COMMENTARY

At the beginning of this scene, the alteration in O'Donnell's speech characteristics, now that the rebellion has failed, is entire. Previously his language was defined by a bombastic exaggeration, akin to the drum-rolling speech of a theatrical ringmaster. Now he is utterly deflated. The superlatives and repetitions of O'Donnell's previous statements – 'big news — huge news — enormous news!' (p. 30) – are replaced by cautious understatements. His entrances onstage had previously been marked by great noise and excitement. Now O'Donnell announces himself with the quiet statement 'it's only

CONTEXT

The Sperrin mountains cover a vast region of Ireland north of Dungannon. They are high and inhospitable, even today.

 CHECK THE BOOK

In Kilroy's 1962 play, *The O'Neill*, the English Lord Deputy, Mountjoy, declares prior to Kinsale that 'we have bribed an Irish chieftain, one Brian MacHugh Og MacMahon, with whiskey ... he says O'Neill cannot restrain the Irish'. In *Making History*, when O'Donnell suggests that 'we were betrayed at Kinsale! ... Brian Og McMahon slipped them the word!' (p. 44), O'Neill dismisses the suggestion.

CONTEXT

In history, O'Donnell left Ireland for Spain in order to try to procure support for a renewed rebellion. He died there, and is suspected to have been poisoned by an English spy. Friel presents a very different picture, in which O'Donnell leaves Ireland out of sadness, and aimlessly plans to go 'wherever the ship takes me. Maybe Spain' (p. 47).

CHECK THE BOOK

In Irish literature, the nation is often personified as a woman. W. B. Yeats's play, *Cathleen Ni Houlihan*, 1902, represents Ireland as Cathleen.

me' (p. 43). He repeats the phrase 'I suppose …' (p. 43), indicating that doubt and guesswork now define his thoughts, rather than certainty and knowledge. Even O'Donnell's physical behaviour marks the contrast in his attitude. Where previously he had bounced around the stage, embracing different characters, pouring wine and gesticulating wildly, now *'he throws himself on the ground and spreads out in exhaustion'* (p. 43).

O'Donnell describes what he's seen throughout the country, the famine, begging, and violence perpetrated by the English forces under Lord Mountjoy. He emphasises, however, that much of his information derives from hearsay. O'Donnell repeats the phrases 'my mother says' (p. 44), 'do you know what I heard?' (p. 44), and 'what everybody at home's saying' (p. 45). The fact that he admits his knowledge is based on hearsay, diminishes O'Donnell's own authority as a historical witness. Even after the initial diminishment of O'Donnell's bombast in this scene, the old drum-rolling tendency returns to him, and he cries 'wait till you hear this, Hugh' (p. 44). However, substance is, and always has been, lacking in O'Donnell's speech. This is reinforced by his delay in responding to O'Neill's direct questions.

O'Donnell's confidence breaks down further. This is emphasised by an **oxymoronic** stage direction that instructs him to smile *'resolutely and uncertainly'* (p. 47) at the same time. The direction reveals the dualism that has defined O'Donnell throughout the play. Uncertainty and insubstantiality have lain at the heart of his bombastic expressions of resolution. The dualism is continued by the combination of humour and sadness that characterise O'Donnell's behaviour here. One moment he laughs and jokes (p. 47), the next he is *'about to break down, he flings his arms around O'Neill. They embrace for several seconds. Then O'Donnell goes to his bag for a handkerchief'* (p. 48). O'Donnell's devastation at what has happened to Ireland is revealed when he personifies the nation as a 'goddess' (p. 47). Ireland is represented in the **microcosm** of a lover. Politics are felt on an intensely personal level, and O'Donnell's patriotic feelings are interwoven with his most intimate emotions.

ACT II SCENE 1 [PP. 48–54]

- To O'Donnell, O'Neill explains his decision to make a public declaration of loyalty to Elizabeth I, Queen of England, and to surrender all his lands, all his 'political and military power' (p. 49).
- Harry informs O'Neill and O'Donnell that Peter Lombard has moved permanently to Rome, where the Pope has invented 'some sort of job for him' (p. 51).
- Harry also has to relate the devastating news that both Mabel and her newborn son have died in childbirth.

CONTEXT

The 'strange-looking biscuits' (p. 51) which Harry brings may refer to the battle of the Ford of the Biscuits in 1594, when O'Donnell defeated an English force. The battle was named after the English supplies that covered the area afterwards.

Despite the failure of his attempted rebellion, O'Neill is still torn between duty to the Irish, and duty to the English. Mabel has been advising him to 'make a public declaration of loyalty to the Queen' (p. 48), and plead for reinstatement as the Earl of Tyrone. O'Donnell is horrified by this thought, and becomes more so when he and O'Neill take it in turns to read out the draft of his submission.

Harry Hoveden returns from having accompanied Mabel to her safe house. He brings food, drink, and news concerning Peter Lombard's escape to Rome. Harry informs O'Neill that

Sir Garret Moore – who had invited O'Neill for 'a few days' fishing' at his home at Mellifont Abbey at the start of the play (p. 3) – wants to help to reconcile O'Neill with the English crown. Harry also brings news regarding a recent upsurge in the number of histories of Ireland that are being written. The most important, and devastating, news that Harry brings, however, concerns Mabel. She and her newborn son have died, shortly after childbirth, of 'poisoning of the blood' (p. 53).

COMMENTARY

When O'Neill describes Mabel's advice to him to 'pick up the pieces, start all over again', O'Donnell comments that 'she's a very loyal wee girl' (p. 48). The word 'loyal' carries great resonance in *Making History*, and is considered in the **Themes** section alongside such similar terms as 'duty', 'piety', and 'faith'. The play repeatedly questions to whom O'Neill should demonstrate loyalty, the Irish or the English. The play also explores the historian's and the playwright's divided loyalties between the demands of fiction and the demands of historical fact. O'Donnell's description of 'loyal' Mabel at this point is loaded. Politically, a person who supports the English crown, and the union of England and Ireland, is described as a Loyalist. Is Mabel, then, privately loyal to her chosen husband, or politically Loyal to her New English heritage? A Loyalist could not also be wholly loyal to O'Neill.

O'Neill has written a submission to Queen Elizabeth, in the hope that she might reinstate him as Earl of Tyrone, albeit 'with only nominal authority, without political or military power whatever' (p. 48). O'Donnell and O'Neill take it in turns to read O'Neill's submission to Queen Elizabeth. O'Donnell's good humour fades as it is read out, and the force of O'Neill's defeat becomes clear. There is a detailed analysis of the submission in **Extended commentaries**, Text 3 – Act II scene 1 (pp. 48–50).

Upon his return, Harry mentions that there has been a recent upsurge in the number of histories written about Ireland in recent years. He mentions the name of Tadhg O Cianain, referring to the writer of an eyewitness Gaelic account of the Flight of the Earls from Ireland to exile in Europe. It is **anachronistic** that Harry mentions this now, before the Flight of the Earls has taken place in the play. O'Neill is still in Ireland at this point. Harry also mentions 'an Englishman called Spenser' (p. 52), whose book is gaining much attention from the English government. This refers to Edmund Spenser and his *View of the State of Ireland*, 1633. Spenser's *View of the State of Ireland* was fiercely anti-Irish, and defined its Gaelic inhabitants by their 'barbarous rudenes'. Although the *View* wasn't published until 1633, it was completed in manuscript form before 1598 – three years before the real battle of Kinsale – and circulated widely. Friel's dating is distorted in this scene. According to the stage directions, this scene takes place in 1593, eight years before the real Kinsale, and five years before the completion of the *View*. Friel's use of real historical documents serves to confuse the story, rather than provide clarification. A more detailed discussion of Friel's extensive distortions of history in *Making History* takes place in **Themes**.

The scene ends with Harry's horrible task of informing O'Neill of the death of Mabel and her son, shortly after childbirth. Her final words, as described in the play, were that 'Hugh would never betray his people' (p. 53). The question of where her loyalty lies appears to be resolved. Harry tells O'Neill that 'the doctor said something about poisoning of the blood' (p. 53). Poisoning was mentioned much earlier in the play, in Act I scene 1, when O'Donnell suggested poisoning O'Doherty. A poisoned body can be a **microcosmic** representation of a country falling apart on the inside, after the intrusion of a malign influence. This could represent Ireland dying, 'poisoned' by the intrusion of Englishness. The notion of poisoned blood is a meaningful one. Prior to the **Renaissance**, arguments for preventing the intermarrying of Gaelic and English communities sought to keep the respective bloodlines 'pure'. This is similar to Mary's attempts in Act I scene 2 to stop the fennel and dill seeds cross-fertilising and resulting in 'a seed that's neither one thing or the other' (p. 22). Mabel's poisoned blood may represent her marriage to O'Neill, the intermarrying of English and Gaelic bloodlines. That she was poisoned by this marriage implies that any hopes of amicable Anglo-Irish cohabitation have decisively failed. The death of the son of Mabel and O'Neill seals the loss of hope.

CONTEXT

In contrast to Spenser, Francis Bacon argued for 'a plantation in a pure soil; that is, where a people are not displanted to the end to plant in others. For else it is rather an extirpation than a plantation', 'Of Plantations', (1625).

Lady Penelope
Rich was forced
into an arranged
marriage with
Lord Rich. In 1590,
Charles Blount,
Lord Mountjoy,
became her lover,
and she had six
children by him.
Lord Rich put up
with the adultery,
as he was in awe
of Lady Penelope's
brother. When her
brother died, Lord
Rich threw Lady
Penelope out.
When Mountjoy
returned from
Ireland in 1603,
she moved in with
him, living in open
adultery.

GLOSSARY

52	Lady Penelope Rich Lord Mountjoy's long-term mistress
52	Edmund Spenser a courtier, politician and poet, best known for his long poem *The Faerie Queen*, 1590
53	Tabhair Dom Do Lamh 'Give Me Your Hand' – the name of an Irish harp tune by Ruadhaire Dall O Cathain. Also a possible reference to the Red Hand of Ulster, the image present on the seals and shields of the kings of Ulster

ACT II SCENE 2 [PP. 54–60]

- *'Many years'* (p. 54) have passed and it is the early 1610s. The Flight of the Earls has taken place, and O'Neill is living in Rome, in exile from Ireland.
- O'Donnell is dead, and O'Neill is living with Harry, Lombard and O'Neill's fourth wife, Catriona.
- O'Neill has become the 'soured émigré' he once predicted O'Donnell might become. He drinks too much, and his temper is described as *'volatile and bitter and dangerous'* (p. 54). Upon hearing he's run out of money, O'Neill accuses Harry of betraying him.

The scene begins with O'Neill's entrance onstage after a day's drinking. He begins reading Lombard's history of himself, and becomes angry at Lombard's distortion of his identity. When Harry enters, he informs O'Neill that Spain has replied to his letter requesting further help for Ireland. Spain has signed a peace treaty with England, and is currently unable to take part in any plans for a future rebellion.

O'Neill describes his day. He financially survives through pensions granted by the Pope and the Spanish Embassy, and he has been to collect those. He has also spent time with a prostitute, Maria, and has been drinking with two other Irish émigrés. The three men are planning a renewed rebellion in Ireland, but O'Neill's inebriated and bitter description of their plans sounds farcical in the extreme. O'Neill wants to continue drinking, but Harry informs him there's no wine, and he's run out of money. O'Neill accuses Harry of spending the money on himself, and of betraying him.

COMMENTARY

The stage descriptions for this scene are strikingly similar to those for the first scene. O'Neill's room is *'scantily furnished'* (pp. 1, 54) in both, and the same table, chairs and stool are present. The *'comfortless'* furnishings reflect O'Neill's unhappy state of mind. In the first scene, the lack of homeliness of Dungannon Castle represented O'Neill's **metaphorical** homelessness, his position caught between two loyalties. In this scene, it represents his literal exile. O'Neill is clearly lost when he comes onstage. He – perhaps humorously – mistakes a stool for a passer-by, and requests directions to his residence. In his drunken state, O'Neill inhabits a borderland between fiction and reality, similar to that described by the half-sighted half-blind heroine of Friel's play *Molly Sweeney*, 1994: 'what I think I see may be fantasy or indeed what I take to be imagined may very well be real.' O'Neill's eyesight is fading too (p. 54). This could be understood as a madness induced by subjective thought: any grip on reality has been lost amongst subjective interpretations. O'Neill's use of Italian and Spanish in this scene reinforces the sense of his disorientation. He has lost the important link between his language and his identity. When O'Neill finally lifts his taper and realises that he's in 'the right building indeed' (p. 55), his reference to it as 'home' sounds highly **ironic**. O'Neill is clearly not at home, in himself or in Rome.

The directions regarding props and lighting for this scene ensure that Lombard's history book occupies a central position. Initially, the *'only light on stage'* (p. 54) illuminates the *'large book – the history'*, and when O'Neill enters, he brings his *'lighted taper'* up to it, and *'leans over the page, his face close to it'* (p. 55). He begins reading from it. The text that O'Neill recites is taken almost word for word from an early seventeenth-century biography of Hugh O'Donnell, Lughaidh O'Clery's *The Life of Hugh Roe O'Donnell*, 1603. Lombard will refer to this book when he enters later in the scene (p. 64). What might be the purpose of Friel's appropriation of

CONTEXT

Neachtain O Domhnaill, who O'Neill has been drinking with, was characterised by one of his acquaintances as 'the wickedest boy he ever dealt with in all his life'. He died in the Tower of London in 1624. Christopher Plunkett, O'Neill's other drinking partner, who was a member of an Old English family, left Ireland with the Flight of the Earls.

? QUESTION

Making History opposes a **subjective** understanding of history, in which there are many possible interpretations of the facts, to an **objective** understanding, in which there is only one 'reality'. Which idea of history-writing do you support?

O'Clery's celebration of O'Donnell, for a celebration of O'Neill? Firstly, it emphasises the insubstantiality of O'Donnell's character as it is presented throughout *Making History*. Whereas in history there is evidence that O'Donnell was an accomplished fighter and leader, Friel's O'Donnell is an impulsive, often vacuous, character. Friel has stripped him of the historical authority bestowed upon him by O'Clery, by giving it to O'Neill instead. Secondly, it asserts the right of the playwright to distort or 'interpret' history in a subjective manner. The theme of subjective history-writing is explored in **Themes** and **Historiographical background** sections. The misattribution of O'Clery's *Life* belongs to a series of historical distortions and falsifications that occur in *Making History*, which are discussed in **Characterisation, Themes** and **Dramatic techniques**.

O'Neill's speech is characterised by desperate questioning. He wonders 'where … is everybody?' (p. 56), and, when Harry appears, O'Neill continues to interrogate him. This is a parody of the question–answer relationship established by O'Neill and Harry in the first scene of *Making History*. There, O'Neill's questions followed by Harry's answers established the pair as mutually dependent. In this final scene, O'Neill is still desperately dependent upon Harry, but he tries to push him away, and their relationship is disintegrating. O'Neill's questions do not seek information, but are demanding and angry. The disintegration of mutual trust is so extreme that O'Neill accuses Harry of 'spying on me' (p. 57), squandering his money and being disloyal.

This scene is punctuated by meaningful references to the geography of Rome. O'Neill explains – to himself – that he's 'trying to make my way to the Palazzo dei Penitenzieri which is between the Via della Conciliazione and the Borgo Santo Spirito where I live' (p. 54). The Borgo Santo Spirito was an area that had been home to colonies of foreigners and exiles since the eighth century. As an exile himself, it is appropriate for O'Neill to be living there. His reference to the Palazzo dei Penitenzieri draws attention to the resonances of Penitenzieri – penance, penitence and penitents – and suggests that O'Neill regrets his rebellion. The 'Via della Conciliazione' belongs to the list of Brian Friel's distortions of history and reality in *Making History*. The street was actually constructed in 1936, and is

CONTEXT

O'Neill's regret for his rebellion would be ironic. Pope Clement VIII's *Bull of Indulgence* granted forgiveness to all those who took part (p. 33). This section of *Making History* suggests there is a difference between being forgiven, and forgiving oneself.

named after a treaty in 1929 which reconciled the Italian church and
state. Its name – The Road of Reconciliation – alludes to O'Neill's
past hopes of reconciling the Gaelic and English inhabitants of
Ireland, and the Catholic and Protestant churches. When O'Neill
describes his day to Harry, he says that he 'walked to the top of the
Janiculum hill' (p. 67). This hill was named after Janus, the two-
faced Roman god who looked simultaneously to the past and the
future. *Making History* describes O'Neill as an Irish counterpart to
Janus, in his attempt to look to the Gaelic past and the English
future, and his simultaneous loyalty to the crown and to his clan.
Importantly, the Janiculum hill is the location for the Church of San
Pietro in Montario, where the real O'Neill is buried next to his son.
O'Neill's prediction that he'll 'die in this damned town, Harry …
and be buried here, beside my son, in the church of San Pietro'
(p. 57) refers to the historical reality.

O'Neill describes the 'most agreeable hour' he spent with 'Maria the
Neapolitan' (p. 57), who, we assume, is a prostitute. The name
Maria is ironic: it refers to the Virgin Mary, and, we assume, Maria
the Neapolitan is certainly not virginal. The ironies and misnomers
in this scene create the image of a world turned upside down, in
which the wrong words are attached to the wrong objects. O'Neill
points out to Harry that the phrase Maria said to him after
accepting his payment – 'Grazie, signor. Grazie molto' – was
identical to the phrases he himself uttered when accepting his
pensions – 'Grazie. Grazie molto' and 'Gracias, Muchas gracias'
(p. 57). By pointing out that his language is identical to that of a
prostitute, O'Neill implies that their behaviour is comparable too.
Maria prostitutes herself to O'Neill, and O'Neill has prostituted
himself to the Catholic Church and Spain in the name of raising
support for his rebellion. This suggests that he feels that, in his
rebellion, his own interest in the promotion of Gaelic identity
became sidelined by a campaign to support the Catholic Church
and the Spanish Counter-Reformation. O'Neill has acquiesced to
Mabel's earlier suspicion that when Lombard was 'talking about
you and about Ireland, he's really talking in code about Rome and
Roman power' (p. 39).

CONTEXT

The Borgo Santo
Spirito gets its
name from the
oldest hospital in
the city of Rome,
which is located
there. The
hospital, built in
AD 727 was
designed to offer
care and sanctuary
for the pilgrims
visiting the city.

GLOSSARY

54   Bella ... bellissima Italian for 'beautiful' and 'the most
        beautiful'

54   Palazzo dei Penitenzieri, Via della Conciliazione, Borgo Santo
        Spirito situated in the area of Rome surrounding the
        Vatican. The names mean the 'palace of penitents' and
        'the road of reconciliation'

55   vespers evening prayer service in the Roman Catholic Church

56   inacción Spanish for 'inaction'

57   Janiculum hill a hill in Rome, the centre for the cult of
        Janus, the two-faced Roman god

57   Grazie. Grazie molto ... Gracias, Muchas gracias Italian and
        Spanish for 'thank you ... many thanks'

58   Delirium tremens alcohol withdrawal symptoms.
        Technically, it refers to the most severe form of alcohol
        withdrawal, but is often used to refer to lesser cases,
        including tremor, anxiety, nausea and insomnia

CONTEXT

Lombard refers to O'Neill's inauguration at 'the crowning stone at Tullyhogue outside Dungannon' (p. 64). The inauguration of The O'Neill, the head of the clan, traditionally took place at Tullyhogue Fort, the clan seat of the O'Hagans, who were hereditary stewards to the O'Neills. The inauguration stone was embedded in a stone coronation chair, and had been blessed by St Patrick. Hugh O'Neill became The O'Neill in 1593, the last inauguration to occur here before Mountjoy smashed the stone in 1602.

ACT II SCENE 2 [PP. 60–71]

- Lombard enters in the middle of O'Neill and Harry's argument. He describes the underlying theory for his history of O'Neill. This is the most important scene in *Making History*, in terms of its discussion of the practice of history-writing.

- Lombard wants to write O'Neill's story as a heroic national myth. O'Neill wants him to write a faithful record of events, to be honest about the defeat at Kinsale, and to recognise Mabel's crucial importance to his decisions.

- O'Neill believes in the idea of an 'honest' history. Lombard believes there are many different ways to interpret the facts.

- The scene, and the play, ends with a direct clash of these beliefs. Lombard recites the opening of his celebratory history of O'Neill, whilst O'Neill recites his defeated submission to Queen Elizabeth I.

Lombard interrupts O'Neill and Harry's argument and enters holding a bottle of poitín. Lombard asks O'Neill to allow him to check some facts for his history. O'Neill instead interrogates Lombard regarding how he, and Mabel, will be represented in the book. It becomes evident that the two men have very different interpretations of the practice of history-writing, and very different interpretations of the centrality of Mabel to the rebellion. O'Neill perceives Mabel to be 'central' (p. 62), but Lombard argues that she 'didn't reroute the course of history' and is relatively marginal (p. 68) to events. O'Neill perceives Kinsale to be a 'disgrace' (p. 65), but Lombard wants to represent the battle as 'a triumph', 'the crushing of the most magnificent Gaelic army ever assembled' (p. 65).

The discussion between Lombard and O'Neill becomes a 'battle' and O'Neill defines it as his 'last battle' (p. 63). Lombard asserts his right to interpret the facts in his own way, and to write the rebellion – and O'Neill – into a nationalist myth of which the Irish people can be proud. O'Neill wants his *whole* life' (p. 63) to be recorded, and an honest representation to be constructed of his, and his rebellion's, failings. The play ends with these two desires articulated simultaneously, as Lombard recites the opening of his celebratory history, and O'Neill recites the defeated submission he offered to Elizabeth I in 1603. O'Neill clearly loses the 'battle', however, and ends the play in tears.

COMMENTARY

When Lombard comes onstage, he is carrying a bottle of 'Waterford poitín' (p. 60). Poitín is a clear Irish spirit made from grain, and Waterford is famous for being the poitín capital of Ireland. Waterford is also the historical Lombard's birthplace, and he refers to it as 'my own parish' (p. 61). The poitín gives Lombard the opportunity to make a pun on the word 'spirit', playing on its double-meaning of spirit/alcohol and spirit/spirituality. A pun is humorous because it contains two meanings within one word. It is the verbal equivalent of a divided personality, like O'Neill's. In fact, the poitín comes from a divided town, 'a very remote place called Affane, about ten miles from Dungarvan' (p. 61). Lombard describes Affane as 'an annex of heaven – or Hades' (p. 61), for it has a simultaneously heavenly and hellish nature. In 1564, Affane was the scene of a battle between the Earls of Desmond and Ormond, in which Ormond – whose descendant Lombard

> **CONTEXT**
>
> Lombard's pun on 'spirit' refers back to an earlier moment in *Making History*, in Act I scene 2. In response for O'Neill's demand for a Bull of Excommunication from the Pope, Lombard argued that 'excommunication is a spiritual matter' (p. 37). O'Neill replied that 'the situation is as "spiritual" now as it was twenty years ago'. Friel's play questions the nature of spirituality.

remembers (p. 61) – was defeated. It is a town in which the divisions between the Gaelic clans was clear.

O'Neill and Harry speak respectively in questions and answers, and demonstrate their mutual dependency. On the other hand, Lombard is entirely self-sufficient, and this is demonstrated in his speech. Lombard talks to himself, asking himself questions and answering them before anyone else has had a chance: 'I've come at a bad moment, have I? No? Good' (p. 60). This exhibits Lombard's egocentricism, his self-absorption, and his single-minded interest in his history-writing project. His speech is self-reflexive, it comments on itself. For example, after referring to 'my history', Lombard proceeds to analyse his own speech: '"my history"! You would think I was Thucydides, wouldn't you' (p. 61). Albeit jokingly, Lombard here compares himself to a well-known classical historian, Thucydides, who is best known for his *History of the Peloponnesian War*. This shows the high regard in which he holds himself.

This is the most important scene in *Making History*'s discussion of historical method. Lombard and O'Neill set out their understandings of historiography. O'Neill believes in 'truth', and in the possibility of that truth being faithfully represented. Lombard is a relativist. This means that he believes only in interpretations of events, and that there is not a single 'right' version of the 'truth'. He therefore asserts his right to represent O'Neill as a national hero, and to sideline Mabel's importance, despite O'Neill's different interpretation of facts. Importantly, Lombard and O'Neill use similar phrases in their descriptions of history-writing but with radically different meanings. For example both characters define their intent to represent 'the *whole* life' (pp. 62–3). O'Neill uses pronouns to distance himself from Lombard's history. He uses the demonstrative pronoun 'that' – 'that [*book*] … that thing there' (p. 63) – which is a form of **deixis**. 'That' is a pointing word, and O'Neill establishes distance between himself and the book by pointing away. O'Neill reverses the possessive pronouns articulated by Lombard to deny any relationship between himself and the history. When Lombard refers to the book as 'your history', O'Neill emphasises it is '*your* history' (p. 63). This is the reverse of a grammatical technique employed by Mabel in Act I scene 1. She began using the personal pronoun 'we' to refer to the 'O'Neills',

CONTEXT

Thucydides was born around 460 BC and died around 400 BC, in Greece. His book, the *History of the Peloponnesian War*, describes the war between Sparta and Athens in the fifth century BC, and is widely thought to be the first history text of its kind.

not the 'Upstarts', demonstrating her changed allegiance. Whereas Mabel used pronouns to exhibit inclusion, in this final scene, O'Neill uses pronouns to exclude himself from Lombard's history.

The differences between Lombard and O'Neill's versions of history come into conflict at the end of this scene, at the end of the play. Lombard recites the opening of his history of O'Neill, whilst O'Neill declares his submission to the English, written back in 1603. Lombard's presentation exhibits a 'God-like prince' (p. 71), O'Neill's exhibits a cowed, defeated, sad old man. In fact, the text that Lombard recites is not a biography of O'Neill at all, but a biography of Hugh O'Donnell. He had mentioned the book earlier in the scene: 'Ludhaidh O'Cleary has written a life of Hugh' (p. 64). Lombard's recitation entirely derives from O'Clery's book, which was published in 1603. Why should Friel choose to use a biography of Hugh O'Donnell in a supposed celebration of Hugh O'Neill? It is consistent with Friel's representation of O'Donnell throughout *Making History*. Whereas there is evidence that the historical O'Donnell was a competent leader and brave soldier, Friel's O'Donnell is oddly vacuous and trivial. The existence of a celebratory biography of O'Donnell might have appeared incongruous in the face of Friel's representation. The final scene, in which Lombard reads his biography 'by heart' whilst the book remains shut, has a strange effect (p. 70). Ultimately, neither the audience of *Making History* nor O'Neill knows what Lombard's book really contains. The book stays shut. Lombard professes to read his history by heart, but when he recites, we hear another man's biography of a different subject. The play ends with Lombard's book shut, private and unknown.

CHECK THE BOOK

In *Faber Critical Guides: Brian Friel*, 2000, Nesta Jones describes O'Donnell as 'a bit of a clown'.

GLOSSARY	
60	poitin a clear Irish spirit made from grain. Pronounced potch-een
61	Hades ancient Greek world of the dead, the underworld
67	the Four Evangelists Matthew, Mark, Luke and John, the authors of the New Testament gospels which offer narratives of Christ's life
70	chianti an Italian red wine

EXTENDED COMMENTARIES

Three passages have been selected from *Making History* to illustrate different aspects of the play, such as language and style, characterisation, staging and performance techniques, and recurrent themes and techniques.

TEXT 1 – ACT I SCENE 1 (PP. 1–4)

From 'Tell me the name of these again' to stage directions '(O'NEILL *stops working*.)'

The first scene of *Making History* is concerned with beginnings: the beginning of the play, and the beginning of the life of 'young Brian's first child' (p. 1). Both beginnings take place through words. The play is constituted of words. Brian's child will be given a name at 'a big christening party' (p. 1). In this scene, the emphasis on beginning-through-naming coincides with the onstage presence of a large amount of flowers. Every stage direction in this section concerns O'Neill's flowers. Initially, Hugh O'Neill is '*inexpertly cutting the stems off flowers, thrusting the flowers into various vases and then adding water*' (p. 1). Shortly after, the flowers are named and O'Neill '*silently mouths the word* Genista *again and then continues distributing the flowers*' (p. 2). Moments later, he '*goes off to get more flowers*' and '*enters again with an armful of flowers*' (p. 2). While Harry Hoveden talks, O'Neill '*continues with his flowers*' (p. 3), and repeatedly '*returns to his flowers*' (p. 4). He only '*stops working*' (p. 4) when he is distracted by the news that 'young Essex's been arrested and thrown in the Tower' (p. 4). After this point, O'Neill's stage directions concern props other than flowers, such as '*a large pile of papers*' (p. 4) and '*the letter*' (p. 5) from Henry Bagenal. The armfuls of flowers that O'Neill distributes around the room have a prominent physical presence in *Making History*'s first scene. They are the only decoration in an otherwise '*scantily furnished*' (p. 1) and undecorated set. They are also verbally prominent, and dominate the subject-matter of seventeen exchanges of dialogue in this first section. They recur later in Act I scene 1 when Mabel enters for the first time. What might be the significance of these flowers in these important first moments of the play?

The flowers are named as 'Spanish broom' (p. 2), or, in Latin, '*genista*' (p. 1). The naming of the flowers coincides with the naming of 'young Brian's first child' (p. 1). In the Bible, the naming of plants is the first naming ritual in history: the naming of plants can therefore be said to be the archetypal naming ritual. At the beginning of the Bible's first book, Genesis, God and Adam bestow names on to the flora and fauna of the Garden of Eden. In *Making History* the flowers are important for the resonances they bring to the other naming rituals. They are also important for their own names.

The flowers are called 'Spanish broom'. The presence of the 'Spanish' broom on stage anticipates the Spanish presence in Ireland, supporting O'Neill's troops. Harry translates the name into Latin as 'genista'. He remembers that 'Virgil mentions it somewhere' (p. 1). Harry has clearly received a classical education. Harry is Anglo-Irish, but his classical education contradicts the stereotypical opinion, expressed in Act I scene 2 by Mary, that the Irish and their sympathisers are 'savage people' (p. 24). In fact, Virgil mentions Spanish broom in his *Georgics*. The *Georgics* are poems that celebrate the rural world as a retreat from, and a commentary upon, the horror of civil war. The broom often becomes endangered by new additions to its habitat, which might 'stifle its growth, dry up its fruitfulness' (Virgil, *The Eclogues, Georgics and Aeneid of Virgil*, translated by C. Day Lewis, 1966, pp. 69–71). Friel evokes Virgil to describe the civil war within Ireland. For him, the Spanish broom represents the indigenous Irish inhabitants threatened by the newly-planted English 'Upstarts'.

Virgil was not alone in exploiting broom's significance. Walter Scott, in *The Talisman*, 1832, introduced broom as a component of the heraldic badge of the house of Plantagenet (of which the English king, Richard I, was a member). In Scott's novel, broom is interpreted as an ancient 'emblem of humility'. It is an **ironic** emblem, however: Richard I showed no humility in his violent colonial exploits during the Crusades. Broom becomes an emblem of English hypocrisy, of acts of barbaric violence carried out under a veneer of politeness and decorum. This is described later in Act I scene 1 of *Making History*. Hugh O'Donnell refers

CHECK THE BOOK

In Friel's play *Translations* the Irish characters are almost as happy conversing in Latin and Greek as in Gaelic. Hugh suggests that 'our own culture and the classical tongues made a happier conjunction' (p. 23) than the link between Gaelic and English. The classical learning of these rural characters far exceeds that of the English surveyors, who speak neither Latin nor Greek, and repeatedly confuse the sounds of Latin and Gaelic.

CHECK THE BOOK

O'Neill's dual allegiance to the English and the Irish has been perceived by the historian R. F. Foster as representative of 'the Janus-face of Ireland' (*Modern Ireland: 1600–1972*, 1987, p. 4), referring to the two-faced Italian deity. Mary alludes to this two-facedness when she states that O'Neill 'bows and scrapes before the Lord Deputy in Dublin ... and the very next day he's plotting treason with Spain' (p. 25).

to Sir Henry Bagenal as 'Butcher Bagenal' indicating his barbaric 'raiding and plundering' (p. 14) beneath the façade of the 'cold pragmatism of the Renaissance mind' (p. 28). The charge of two-facedness, or Janus-facedness, is levelled at the English *and* O'Neill.

The flowers precede Mary's gift of packets of seeds to Mabel in Act I scene 2. The seeds should be understood in conjunction with the many references to plantation in that scene. As the **Themes** section explains, the establishment of New English families on Irish land was called plantation. The planting of seeds in Irish soil is a **metaphor** for the plantation of English settlers in Ireland. O'Neill holds fully-grown flowers, whereas Mary carries ungerminated seeds. This represents the longevity of O'Neill's Irish heritage as opposed to the newness of the English presence in Ireland. Like the ungerminated seeds, the 'upstart' English haven't yet flourished in the Irish soil. Flowers, though, have a limited lifespan. The Spanish broom is in full bloom at the start of *Making History*, and this coincides with the play's setting at the height of summer, in '*late August*' (p. 1). The flowers will fade however, summer will turn to winter, and O'Neill's ascendancy will diminish. The seeds and the New English, however, will flourish.

TEXT 2 – ACT I SCENE 2 (PP. 34–5)

From: 'I'm remembering Sir Henry Sidney' to 'But all of that is of no interest'

This section of *Making History* takes place after Lombard and O'Donnell's news that Spain is providing military and financial support for O'Neill's rebellion. It occurs before O'Neill has decided how to react to this news. It is a bridge between these two sections, a pause in which O'Neill may stop and think, before taking action. It may be called a structural **hiatus**. In this section O'Neill's **soliloquy** allows the audience a glimpse of his private self. In the case of Hugh O'Neill, this is a rare privilege. There are very few instances where the audience, or the other characters of *Making History*, witness the secret feelings present within this '*private, sharp-minded man*' (p. 1). That Hugh O'Neill's **monologue** is intended as a soliloquy is indicated by the stage directions, '*he speaks very softly, almost as if he were talking to himself*' (p. 34).

The first sentence of the speech uses a grammatical tense called the continuous present. O'Neill says 'I'm remembering' as opposed to 'I remember' (p. 34), the simple present tense. The effect of this use of the continuous present is to illustrate the internal workings of O'Neill's mind as they happen. It increases the audience's sense of access into O'Neill's private mental universe. The words 'remember' and 'memories' are repeated four times in the first sentences of the soliloquy. Memories are private events, peculiar to the individual. Again, this emphasises the fact that O'Neill is revealing his private identity.

The subject of O'Neill's soliloquy is his memory of his childhood spent with the Sidneys, an aristocratic family in England. In history, Sir Henry Sidney (1529–86) was embroiled in Irish politics. He was the Lord Deputy of Ireland between 1565 and 1571, during which time he was responsible for the imposition of English law and culture. In 1571 Sidney left his post, resenting Elizabeth I's failure to support him. He was reinstated in 1575, but left again in 1578. Sidney then moved to his Ludlow estate – the 'great castle at Ludlow in Shropshire' (p. 34) mentioned by O'Neill – to act as President of Wales. Henry Sidney was the father of Philip Sidney – described by O'Neill as 'younger than I' (p. 34) – who became one of the best-known writers of the Tudor court.

> **CONTEXT**
>
> Philip Sidney is most famous for his prose piece *A Defense of Poesy*, and his long work, *The Old Arcadia*.

Whether O'Neill spent his childhood with the Sidneys in England is a matter of debate for historians. Sean O'Faolain's history *The Great O'Neill*, 1942, was Friel's chief source for *Making History*. O'Neill's description of his English residence is clearly taken from O'Faolain's book. O'Neill describes 'the orchards; and the deerpark; and those enormous fields of wheat and barley' (p. 34). This is similar to O'Faolain's description of 'the fine game-preserves, the deerpark' and 'the fishponds, the flower-gardens, the orchards'. O'Neill also remembers that 'Drake was there once, I remember. And Frobisher and his officers on the eve of their first South American voyage' (p. 34). O'Faolain suggests that the historical O'Neill 'could have stood at the waterside to see Frobisher set out on one of his annual expeditions to Africa and the

CHECK THE NET

For biographies of Francis Drake and Martin Frobisher, go to **www.channel4.com** and type 'pirates' into the search engine.

Levant, or young Drake set off with the buccaneers for the Spanish Main'. These passages refer to Sir Francis Drake and Martin Frobisher, two of the most famous Elizabethan explorers who established English colonies abroad. By juxtaposing these overseas explorers with Sir Henry Sidney, *Making History* suggests that the practices of the three men are comparable. Sidney's imposition of English law in Ireland might exhibit the same 'naked brutality and imperial greed' (p. 34) as Frobisher's colonisation of South America.

There are historians who do not believe that O'Neill spent any time with the Sidneys. Hiram Morgan in particular criticises O'Faolain's description of O'Neill's childhood for its 'wild inaccuracy, crass romanticism and faulty revisionism'. Morgan states that, 'unable to reject the received notion of O'Neill's education in England, [O'Faolain] embroidered it with fanciful references to life at the Court and country houses of Elizabethan England'. Brian Friel, however, is less concerned with historical veracity, than with the construction of Hugh O'Neill as a mythical figure.

In the soliloquy, O'Neill remembers that 'every evening after dinner Sir Henry would propose a topic for discussion: *Travel – Seditions and Troubles – Gardens – Friendship and Loyalty – Good Manners – The Planting of Foreign Countries*' (p. 34). These topics are the titles of essays by one of the most prominent English thinkers of the Renaissance period, Francis Bacon. In 1625 Bacon published his *Essays, or Counsels Civil and Moral*, which included short discussions of subjects such as 'Of Travel', 'Of Seditions and Troubles', 'Of Gardens', 'Of Friendship' and 'Of Plantations'. Bacon advocates England's planting of colonies abroad and argues that 'plantations are amongst ancient, primitive, and heroical works'. However, Bacon did warn against colonisers 'displanting' the original inhabitants, or filling the country with 'too many counsellors'.

Bacon's encouragement of English colonisation is shared by Sir Henry Sidney. At the end of his soliloquy, O'Neill describes how Sidney drunkenly quoted from a friend's letter that 'those Irishmen who live like subjects play but as the fox which when you have him on a chain will seem tame; but if he ever gets loose, he will be wild again' (p. 35). Sidney and Trollope are suggesting that any display of English loyalty from an Irishman is a deception. Deep down, the Irish remain 'wild' and opposed to 'the calculation, good order, common sense, the cold pragmatism of the Renaissance mind' (p. 28). The animal **metaphors** used here compare the Irish character to primitive savagery. This view is expressed by Mary Bagenal earlier in *Making History*. The fox imagery is also associated with hunting, a traditional English aristocratic sport. The comparison of the Irish to a fox suggests that they are hunted and victimised by the English. The fox is traditionally thought to be a wily, deceptive animal. This corresponds to O'Neill's shrewd politics, in which, as Mary describes, 'he bows and scrapes before the Lord Deputy in Dublin ... and the very next day he's plotting treason with Spain'. Mary characterises this political practice as 'slippery' (p. 25).

O'Neill's soliloquy ends with his confession that he no longer feels resentment towards Henry Sidney for 'that trivial little hurt' (p. 35). The soliloquy concludes with a sense of private calm, and a *'pause'* (p. 35). The whole soliloquy has been meditative. The repetition of phrases – 'explored and fashioned' (p. 34) is repeated twice – and the frequent use of the co-ordinating **conjunction** 'and' gives O'Neill's speech a smooth, flowing quality. The deep insight of O'Neill's revelations, and our glimpse of his private self, are dramatically counteracted at the end of the soliloquy. O'Donnell noisily interrupts O'Neill. We remember that he wasn't in fact alone on stage at all. At the end of this meditative pause, O'Neill returns to business with a clap of his hands.

TEXT 3 – ACT II SCENE 1 (PP. 48–50)

From: 'What about you? What are you going to do?' to stage directions 'HARRY *enters. He looks quickly first at* O'NEILL'

This extract takes place after the battle of Kinsale. Harry, O'Neill and O'Donnell are in hiding at '*the edge of a thicket somewhere near the Sperrin mountains*' (p. 43). O'Neill and O'Donnell are considering their future in the wake of their rebellion's failure. Archbishop Lombard has been offered a post in Rome. O'Donnell has decided to leave Ireland, too, for 'wherever the ship takes me.

 CHECK THE BOOK

The use of this type of grammar to convey a constant flow of private thoughts became popular in early twentieth century literature. In Virginia Woolf's *Mrs Dalloway*, 1925, many sentences begin with 'and' to create this sense of a constantly thinking mind. A narrative which attempts to recreate internal thought processes is called a 'stream-of-consciousness' narrative. This term is applicable to O'Neill's soliloquy.

Maybe Spain' (p. 47). O'Neill is torn. His 'instinct' is to leave too, but Mabel is urging him 'to hang on, pick up the pieces, start all over again' (p. 48). In the hopes of being 'restored to my base again and to my own people', O'Neill has written a 'declaration of loyalty' to Queen Elizabeth, renouncing any 'political or military power' (p. 48). In this scene, O'Donnell and Lombard take it in turns to read O'Neill's submission. The stage directions describe how this reading should be conducted: '*as they proceed through the document* – O'DONNELL *reading his sections,* O'NEILL *speaking his by heart* – O'DONNELL'S *good humour drains away and he ends up as formal and as grave as* O'NEILL' (p. 49).

QUESTION

Why do you think Brian Friel bases *Making History*'s language on historical sources? How does this practice fit with the play's description of the relationship of history-writing to fact?

The submission that O'Neill and Lombard read aloud is based upon the historical O'Neill's submission to Queen Elizabeth in 1603. Elsewhere in *Making History*, Friel bases his text upon historical documents. For example, in Act I scene 2, when Lombard reads from Pope Clement VIII's *Bull of Indulgence* – 'To the archbishops, bishops, prelates, chiefs, earls, barons and people of Ireland …' (p. 33) – the text derives from the real historical source. The correspondence between O'Neill and Philip II of Spain, as read aloud in *Making History*, is also taken from the historical documents. The real letters are included within Denis Murphy's introduction to the 1893 edition of Lughaidh O'Clery's *Life of Hugh Roe O'Donnell*. Lombard refers to this book on page 64 of *Making History*, and Brian Friel had clearly read it. In the case of O'Neill's submission, its historical source was entitled 'The Humble Submission of the Earl of Tyrone Before the Lord Deputy and Council, at Dublin, the 8th April of 1603'. In history, Hugh O'Neill made his submission to Queen Elizabeth after the defeat of the Gaelic and Spanish forces at the battle of Kinsale. When composing the submission he was unaware that Elizabeth had died a few days earlier, and that the succeeding king, James I, would receive it instead. The historical submission was not composed in hiding in the Sperrin mountains. It was written at the home of Sir Garret Moore, mentioned as a friend of O'Neill's in *Making History*. In fact, when Harry Hoveden re-enters after the reading of the submission, he informs O'Neill that 'Sir Garret Moore wants to get in touch with you … He wants to explore what areas of common interest might still exist between you and the crown' (p. 52).

Sir Garret invites O'Neill to his home, Mellifont Abbey, to meet some civil servants, in the hope of reconciling O'Neill with the English. O'Neill's historical submission became known as the Treaty of Mellifont.

The text of O'Neill's submission in *Making History* is taken almost word for word from the historical submission. Lombard reads that O'Neill offers to 'prostrate' himself at Queen Elizabeth I's 'royal feet' (p. 49). In the historical submission, O'Neill 'prostrates himself at the royal feet of King James'. *Making History*'s O'Neill does 'renounce and abjure all foreign power whatever and all kind of dependency upon the King of Spain' (p. 49). In the historical submission, O'Neill 'renounces all kind of dependency on any foreign power' and 'especially abjures all dependency on the King of Spain'. 'Particularly', *Making History*'s O'Neill promises, 'will I help in the abolishing of all barbarous Gaelic customs which are the seeds of all incivility ... And for the clearing of all difficult passages and place ... Which are the nurseries of rebellion. And I will endeavour to erect ... Civil habitations for myself and for the people of my country to preserve us against any force by the power of the state' (p. 50). In the historical submission, this passage reads as follows, as the historical figure of O'Neill promises:

> the abolishing of all barbarous customs contrary to the laws, being the seeds of all incivility, and for the clearing of difficult passages and places, which are the nurseries of rebellion, wherein he will employ the labours of the people of his country, and will endeavour for himself and the people of his country to erect civil habitations, and such as shall be of greater effect to preserve against any force but the power of the estate.

In the submission, the fictional and the real O'Neill describe their resignation of 'all claim and title to any lands' (p. 49). This means that O'Neill's political power is 'only nominal authority, without political or military power whatever' (p. 48). O'Neill is pleading for his title back, his name as Earl of Tyrone, but without any actual command over his people. This would divide a word from its meaning, a name from its power. Anxiety regarding the division of words from their meanings – or, using **structuralist** terminology, the division of **signifiers** from their **signifieds** – runs through

CHECK THE BOOK
There are further moments in *Making History* when Friel quotes directly from his source material, such as the final scene. In *Translations*, he quotes word for word from George Steiner's study of translational problems, *After Babel*, 1975. In *Philadelphia, Here I Come!* he quotes from Edmund Burke's description of Marie Antoinette in *Reflections on the Revolution in France*, 1790.

CHECK THE BOOK

For an examination of the nature of history-writing, look at Arthur Marwick's *The Nature of History*, 1970.

Making History. O'Neill worries that the words of Lombard's history won't reflect his true identity. O'Donnell's speech serves to drum up excitement, when there is no reason. In *Translations*, the inhabitants of Baile Beag worry that the newly Anglicised place names won't reflect the history of the area. Language is bound up with identity, and the separation of words from their meanings can lead to a loss of identity. A part of O'Neill's identity is lost when Lombard's words fail to represent O'Neill's true self. More of that identity is lost when O'Neill's title no longer provides an accurate description of his political power.

PART THREE

CRITICAL APPROACHES

CHARACTERISATION

THE HISTORICAL FIGURES AND FRIEL'S CHARACTERS

All the characters in *Making History* are based on historical figures who lived in Ireland in the late sixteenth and early seventeenth centuries. As you will see from the **Historical background** section of these Notes, the events described in *Making History* – O'Neill's marriage to Mabel Bagenal, the Spanish support for his rebellion against English Protestant authority in Ireland, the battle of Kinsale, the Flight of the Earls – all happened in history. However, in his dramatic representation of these historical events, Friel distorts the details. Most obvious is his compression of the actual timespan of history into the timespan of the play. Historically, O'Neill and Mabel's wedding took place in 1591 and the battle of Kinsale in 1601. The real historical events spanned a decade. In *Making History*, the wedding does occur in 1591, but Kinsale occurs at some point between 1592 and 1593. A decade is compressed into a couple of years. The same distortion occurs in Friel's representation of the historical characters of Hugh O'Neill, Hugh O'Donnell, Peter Lombard, Harry Hoveden, Mabel and Mary Bagenal.

Friel has distorted historical figures elsewhere in his plays. In *Translations*, he conducted research into some of the real-life directors of the Ordnance Survey's activities in Ireland, Colonel Thomas Colby, and John O'Donovan. John O'Donovan was a scholar into ancient Irish culture, its antiquities, music and language, who hoped his researches would strengthen the Irish sense of identity. Friel has spoken of his realisation that, whilst working on a dramatisation of O'Donovan, he began distorting O'Donovan's 'real' nature in a 'cruel' manner. 'I read into O'Donovan's exemplary career as a scholar and orthographer the actions and perfidy of a quisling [a traitor to one's country] ... Thankfully, that absurd and cruel reading of O'Donovan's character was short-lived. But it soured a full tasting of the man. And O'Donovan appears in the play as a character called Owen.' *Translations'* Owen, with his

CHECK THE NET
The website **www.theflightof theearls.net** relates the history of those involved in O'Neill's rebellion in detail. It may be useful in comparing Friel's characters with their historical counterparts.

**CHECK
THE BOOK**

Friel began his
writing career by
composing short
stories. In his
volume, *A Saucer of
Larks*, the story 'The
Fawn Pup' describes
the narrator's – and
perhaps Friel's –
difficulty in
summing-up his
father. Because the
father was a
schoolteacher, the
narrator explains,
people would
assume he fitted a
certain stereotype.
In fact, 'there were
anomalies in his
make-up that left
him larger than any
pigeonhole'.

torn loyalties between the English and the Irish, and his slap-dash
translations, is very different from the historical O'Donovan.

Why do you feel Friel chooses to distort historical figures in this
way, when creating characters for his plays? Friel's representation of
historical figures is as unrepresentative as Peter Lombard's depiction
of Hugh O'Neill in *Making History*. Friel is enacting Lombard's
own distortion of history. Lombard justifies his distortion by
stating the need for nationalist heroes in the early seventeenth
century. *Making History* was written at a time – the late 1980s – in
which the Northern Irish situation was extremely tense. The critic
Tony Coult, in *About Friel: The Playwright and the Work*, 2003,
explains that 'central to the intense propaganda war between the
IRA and the British state was the creation of mythical figures as
rallying points for recruitment'. The need for nationalist heroes was
as relevant to the period in which the play was written, as it was to
the period in which the play is set. Friel's O'Neill is hardly a hero,
however, but a flawed human character, caught between his divided
loyalties. What type of hero is Friel's O'Neill? This is discussed
later in this section.

Friel's distortion of historical figures is a comment upon the nature
of identity. It is related to his discussion of history-writing. In
Making History, Lombard explains his view that reality is so multi-
dimensional that any representation of the past is necessarily
selective. No history can tell the whole story. Every history is, in
part, a fiction. 'I don't believe that a period of history – a given
space of time – my life – your life – that it contains within it one
"true" interpretation just waiting to be mined', Lombard explains.
'But I do believe that it may contain within it several possible
narratives: the life of Hugh O'Neill can be told in many different
ways' (pp. 15–16). Lombard relates his view of the multi-
dimensional nature of history to the multi-dimensional nature of
human identity. Both are too complex to be represented in entirety.
O'Neill desperately wants this entirety, though, and pleads with
Lombard to 'record the *whole* life' (p. 63). Lombard explains that
each human character has many different aspects. 'What is the
"truth" about Harry?' he questions, and offers a number of
interpretations of the facts of Harry's life. He concludes that 'for all
I know there may be other "truths" about Harry' (pp. 67–8). No

written history can offer the full truth, so every history is, to a certain degree, 'lying' or selective. What, then, does a little falsification of dates or facts matter in a play? The same applies to people.

HUGH O'NEILL AND SEAN O'FAOLAIN

Friel's O'Neill is described as '*a private, sharp-minded man*' (p. 1). His character undergoes swift changes. One moment he may be sarcastic and hurtful, the next regretful and tender. O'Neill's changeability is both his strength and his weakness. It represents his double-sided political identity, which can either be understood as a form of reconciliation between English and Irish differences, or as a form of treachery. O'Neill begins *Making History* in an '*uncharacteristically outgoing and talkative*' (p. 1) state. At the end of the play, he is emotionally and politically defeated, and '*crying*' (p. 71). Throughout the play, he is an intensely private character, who resides behind a number of public faces. O'Neill remains silent while Lombard and O'Donnell chatter around him. Only once, in his soliloquy (pp. 34–5), does the audience glimpse the private man.

The 'real' Hugh O'Neill was born in 1550. Historians' opinions are divided about the amount of time he spent in England during his childhood. Lombard's *Commentarius* comments that O'Neill's 'education … was of such kind that he is most thoroughly versed in the politics and affairs not only of Ireland but also of England'. Hiram Morgan, a modern historian of O'Neill's rebellion, emphasises that this does not mean O'Neill was educated in England. Morgan strongly criticises Sean O'Faolain's idealised account in *The Great O'Neill*, 1942, of O'Neill's education at the Sidneys' estates in England (see **Extended Commentaries**, Text 2 – Act I scene 2 (pp. 34–5)). O'Neill's power as head of his clan was accompanied by power bestowed upon him by the English crown. He was first made Baron of Dungannon, and then Earl of Tyrone. As Gaelic chieftain of the O'Neill clan, and the Earl of Tyrone, O'Neill's loyalties were divided. In 1594, assisted by Hugh O'Donnell, he began a rebellion against the English presence in Ireland. In 1598, at the battle of the Yellow Ford, this rebellion looked likely to succeed, and there was a real prospect of England losing control of Ireland. However, this Gaelic success was followed

---

CONTEXT

In *Tyrone's Rebellion*, 1983, Hiram Morgan dismisses Sean O'Faolain's book as a work of 'faulty revisionism'. Revisionist histories aim to counter established interpretations of historical events. For example, revisionist accounts of Irish history may counter the accepted view that English culture has tended to dominate, economically and socially. There is more about this in **Historiographical background: Revisionist history**.

by Kinsale in 1601, O'Neill's submission to the crown in 1603, and his departure for the continent in 1607. O'Neill died in July 1616, in exile – a 'soured émigré' (p. 63) – in Rome.

In *Making History*, Friel's O'Neill is the focus for an exploration of how mythical heroes are created. Friel's O'Neill is based more upon the figure described in Sean O'Faolain's book *The Great O'Neill*, than any attempt to define the 'real' O'Neill. Friel's O'Neill is based on an openly heroic portrayal of the man, not the man himself. In *The Great O'Neill* we find the suggestion for the composition of *Making History*. 'If anyone wished to make a study of the manner in which historical myths are created he might well take O'Neill as an example', O'Faolain suggests. 'A talented dramatist might write an informative, entertaining, ironical play on the theme of the living man helplessly watching his translation into a star.' O'Faolain's description of O'Neill's childhood at the Sidneys' estates in Ludlow, Shropshire and Penshurst, Kent, clearly influenced Friel's play. Both mention 'the orchards', 'the deerpark', and the presence of Frobisher (p. 34). Phrases in *The Great O'Neill* are placed almost word for word into Friel's O'Neill's mouth. When O'Neill comments on the New English that 'no wonder our poets call them Upstarts' (p. 6), he is quoting from O'Faolain, who explains that 'the Gaelic poets always refer [to the New English] as "upstarts"'. In the first scene of *Making History*, Archbishop Lombard bears the gifts of 'a silver birdcage and a gold and silver candelabra' (p. 7) to O'Neill from the Pope. This is derived from the final section of *The Great O'Neill*. O'Faolain describes O'Neill sitting under the glow of 'the two great wax candles, arabesqued with silver and gold, that Paul V had given him … He would barely hear the flutter of the turtle doves in their corner, muttering in their exquisite cages – another Papal gift'. The last scene of *Making History* dramatises the end of *The Great O'Neill*. O'Faolain describes the drunk O'Neill. His 'fingers touch the Archbishop's manuscript … This is his life, his mind, his soul … every word that he reads is untrue. Lombard has translated him into a star … He has made Life into a Myth … the old, drunken man sobs in his rage'.

Friel also uses the character of O'Neill as an image of a divided loyalty. O'Neill's historical ambivalence between duty to his Gaelic clan and to the English crown is described by Friel's O'Neill. 'Do I

CHECK THE BOOK

Brian Friel: Essays, Diaries, Interviews 1964–1999, 1999, contains useful comments made by Friel, which illuminate aspects of his plays.

keep faith with my oldest friend and ally, Maguire, and indeed with the Gaelic civilization that he personifies?' O'Neill demands of Mary. 'Or do I march alongside the forces of Her Majesty?' (p. 27). In an interview with the BBC, Friel described his attraction to O'Neill's 'capacity to dart into and out of his Gaelic consciousness and his English consciousness, his Gaelic experience and his English experience'. Friel uses O'Neill as an image of a complex, multi-layered personality. In *Making History*, O'Neill is split, between his Englishness and his Irishness, between his public face and his private thoughts. Friel's interest in divided personalities may derive from his own experience (see **Brian Friel's life and work**). He grew up in Derry, in Northern Ireland, which Friel describes in *A Paler Shade of Green* as a divided city. 'There were two aspects to Derry', Friel explains. 'One was of a gentle and, in those days, sleepy town; the other was of a frustrating and frustrated town in which the majority of people were disinherited.' It is understandable why Friel, experiencing such division in his own identity, was drawn to a historical figure famous for his divided loyalty.

HUGH O'DONNELL

The distortions Friel exacts on the figures of O'Neill and Lombard (see below) are the most extensive. His representation of Hugh O'Donnell also warrants attention, and it is useful to compare Friel's O'Donnell with the historical figure. The 'real' O'Donnell was called Hugh Roe O'Donnell, known as Red Hugh, and he lived from around 1571 to 1602. He was brought up by the MacSweeneys, who educated him in warfare, amongst other skills. By 1587 he was betrothed to one of O'Neill's daughters, Rose (O'Neill's second wife was O'Donnell's sister Siobhan). The young O'Donnell was kidnapped by the Lord Deputy in 1587, in a wielding of English authority against the powerful Gaelic families of the north. Hugh managed to escape after many years of captivity. He was left with an abiding hatred of English authority, and a desire to combat it by force. In 1592, O'Donnell succeeded his father to leadership of the O'Donnell clan. He joined up with O'Neill, and began a military campaign to resist English authority in Ireland. Despite some notable successes – most importantly, the battle of the Yellow Ford in 1598, in which the Gaelic forces defeated a four

CHECK THE BOOK

In Friel's play *Philadelphia, Here I Come!*, the central character Gar is divided into two aspects, Public Gar and Private Gar. This shows the multi-layered nature of human personality, the different people we become when alone or in company. It may be impossible to represent the whole person. In *Translations*, Yolland considers whether the private aspect of a person, or a community, can ever be reached. Does the private always remain inaccessible, 'hermetic', sealed-off, he wonders.

CHECK THE BOOK

O'Donnell's speech characteristics are similar to those of Fox Melarkey, the travelling-show's ringmaster, in Friel's play *Crystal and Fox*. Both characters function to drum up excitement and encourage someone to 'belt it out'. Like a circus ringmaster, O'Donnell's speech is all rhetoric – glorious rhetoric – but with no action of his own.

thousand strong English army, and killed, amongst others, Henry Bagenal – O'Donnell and O'Neill were defeated at Kinsale in 1601. O'Donnell died in 1602 in Spain, where he had gone to secure more support. Some historians suggest he was poisoned by an English spy named Blake. O'Donnell has been represented in one biography as 'a mighty, bountiful lord, who upheld good government and enforced the law ... with determination and power of character'. A society was even founded in 1977 to campaign for the beatification of Red Hugh O'Donnell.

The presentation of O'Donnell in *Making History* is somewhat different, to say the least. In *The Crows Behind the Plough*, 1991, the critic Christopher Murray comments that 'O'Donnell, historically, was a capable soldier, whose heroic escape from Dublin Castle on New Year's Day 1592 has lent him legendary status; Friel, who never refers to the incarceration episode, presents him as naïve, gauche, and somewhat idiotic'. Friel's O'Donnell is certainly very different from the historical figure. There are moments when Friel nods to the historical facts – O'Donnell refers to O'Neill's marriage to his sister (p. 7), to the tensions between the O'Doherty clan and the O'Donnell clan (p. 9), to his acquaintance with the MacSweeneys, or 'McSwineys' (pp. 12, 47), and to his son Rory (p. 47). On the whole, though, Friel's O'Donnell is an oddly empty character, stripped of his historical prowess and authority. He is described as 'a very young man' (p. 6). His speech is full of bombast and rhetoric, but contains little information or substance. In Act I scene 2, when Lombard and O'Donnell call on O'Neill, bringing the news of Spain's support for the rebellion, O'Donnell's words drum up anticipation for Lombard's news. However, he does not convey any news himself. He is all talk and no action. The most decisive episode in which Friel strips O'Donnell of his historical authority occurs in the last scene. Lombard's recitation of his celebratory history of O'Neill is, in fact, taken from a biography of O'Donnell. The lines 'He will be a God-like prince/ And he will be king for the span of his life' (p. 71) are taken, along with the other extracts from Lombard's history, from Lughaidh O'Clery's *Life of Hugh Roe O'Donnell, Prince of Tirconnell (1586–1602)*, 1603. Friel appropriates O'Clery's celebration of O'Donnell for his portrayal of O'Neill, and the stage O'Donnell becomes stripped of all prowess.

MABEL AND MARY

Mabel's character is young, but self-assured. She demonstrates a
political acuity that earns O'Neill's respect. Mabel is often nervous
in her new home with Hugh O'Neill, and feels out of place amongst
the Gaelic tribes. However, she has a firm resolve, and attempts to
make O'Neill's house her home. Her strength of character makes
her an endearing character. Mabel's sister, Mary, is less sympathetic.
We feel for her loneliness in Ireland, but whereas Mabel encourages
friendship between the New English and the Irish, Mary carries the
prejudices of her family. She is contemptuous of the Gaelic culture.

In the final scene of *Making History*, O'Neill argues that Mabel is
'central' (p. 63). She is central to his personal history, central to the
history of his rebellion and thus central to the history of Ireland.
Some critics agree with O'Neill, and Christopher Murray has
suggested that the discussion between Mabel and her sister Mary in
Act I scene 2 is 'the key scene in the play'.

Historically, Mabel was the daughter of Nicholas Bagenal, and the
sister of Henry Bagenal, successive Queen's Marshals. Her sister
Mary married Sir Patrick Barnewall, and Mabel married O'Neill in
1591. In *Making History*, Mabel's heritage is a New English one,
but she sympathises with O'Neill and the Irish. Her sister Mary
voices the standard New English perception of the Irish, that they
are 'a savage people' whose 'way of life is doomed' (p. 24). Mary's
view is very similar to that of Edmund Spenser, whose *View of the
State of Ireland* was distributed in 1600 and is referred to on p. 52
of *Making History*. Spenser promoted the violent suppression of
the Catholic Irish by English forces. Mabel, on the other hand,
represents the possibility of the English and Irish residing
peacefully – amicably, even – side by side. In the marriage of the
Gaelic chieftain O'Neill to the New English Mabel, both have
decided to 'marry outside the tribe', as it is described in
Translations, 1980. The inter-marrying of Irish inhabitants with
English settlers was controversial. Between the twelfth and fifteenth
centuries it was illegal, punishable by the death penalty. In
Translations Jimmy Jack Cassidy explains that exogamy – marrying
outside the tribe – can be dangerous, as 'both sides get very angry'.
In *Making History*, Mabel and O'Neill's marriage is denounced by

QUESTION

How are the female
characters in
Making History
portrayed by Friel?

the Irish and the English. Lombard and O'Donnell are initially shocked, Mabel's father leaves no message for her on his deathbed, Henry Bagenal withholds her dowry, and Mary tells Mabel that O'Neill's house 'can never be your home' (p. 24). The marriage is perceived as a betrayal by both sides. Mabel and O'Neill try to make it work, however. Mabel tries to make Dungannon her 'home', and starts to refer to herself as an 'O'Neill', not an 'Upstart' (p. 18). When Mary tells her that different plants shouldn't 'cross-fertilize' – a **metaphor** for interracial marriage – Mabel takes her to task and questions why not (pp. 21–2). The failure of their marriage – historically, Mabel left O'Neill upon discovering he had a number of mistresses – and Mabel's death marks the end of hope for a reconciliation between the English and Irish in the play.

It is worth noting how Friel distorts certain facts concerning the 'real' Mabel Bagenal. In the programme notes to *Making History*, he admits that 'even though Mabel, Hugh's wife, died in 1591, it suited my story to keep her alive for another ten years'. However, even this is a falsification, as the critic Sean Connolly has pointed out. In the programme notes, Friel claims that the real Mabel died in 1591, but that he portrays her as dying in 1601. In fact, the real Mabel died in 1595, and Friel actually portrays her death in 1593 in *Making History*. In every account, history appears differently!

LOMBARD AND THE RECORDERS

The Archbishop Peter Lombard is a sly character. His manner is described as '*careful and exact*' although he is also '*a man of humour and perception*' (p. 6). These characteristics combine to create a man who is suave and rather charming, but untrustworthy. Whereas Harry Hoveden cares for O'Neill's wellbeing, Lombard's concern is mostly for himself. Mabel recognises this (p. 39). He is persuasive, and adept with language. Lombard talks O'Neill around to the prospect of a rebellion, and attempts to convert him to his own version of history-writing.

Lombard is important to *Making History* in his role as a history-writer. The play suggests that the real makers of history might be its recorders, not its perpetrators. Friel's notions of history-writing are explored throughout these Notes and, in particular, in **Themes**. In this section, Lombard's character will be explored in comparison with the other recorders who crop up in Friel's plays.

In a significant number of Friel's plays, the stage action is observed by a character who is in the process of recording and interpreting it. In *Aristocrats*, Hoffnung researches past visitors and inhabitants of Ballybeg Hall. In *The Home Place*, Dr Richard Gore measures the heads of the tenants as part of an anthropometric experiment. In *The Freedom of the City*, 1974, Dr Dodds provides sociological analysis whilst the judge, Lord Widgery, passes judgement on the events of the Civil Rights march. In *Translations*, the recorders hold a central role. The Ordnance Surveyors are recording – and changing – the geographical face of Ireland. Friel tends to look askance at these recorders. In *The Achievement of Brian Friel*, 1992, the writer Fintan O'Toole has commented that 'consistently throughout Friel's plays the writers, the chroniclers, the analysts, and the historians are insufficient, and more or less incapable figures'. Friel's recorders believe in the existence of an objective reality, which can be described using the language of science. This is most evident in the case of the anthropometrist Richard Gore in *The Home Place*. Friel, however, does not believe in the existence of what Peter Lombard might call 'one "true" interpretation just waiting to be mined from life' (p. 15). Friel believes that there are many changeable 'truths', many possible interpretations of fact. A science that pretends to have discovered 'the truth' may be affirming an interpretation. The judge, Lord Widgery, in *The Freedom of the City*, provides an example. He describes his investigation into the Civil Rights march as a 'fact-finding exercise'. Widgery presents the result of his inquiry – that the marchers did shoot at the English army, before the English army shot them dead – as the 'truth'. Widgery's conclusion is not the whole truth, however, but a selective interpretation. *The Freedom of the City*'s multiple narratives beg to differ. Recorders who aspire towards objective 'truth' in Friel's plays are rarely trustworthy. Their research generally conceals personal or political agendas.

Lombard is a different type of commentator to the scientific recorders who people Friel's other plays. O'Neill believes in objective 'truth' (p. 63), not Lombard. Lombard is acutely aware that every history, every scientific account, offers only one possible

CONTEXT

The failings of Widgery's inquiry were recognised. A second inquiry – the Saville Inquiry – was commissioned by Tony Blair in 1998 to reassess the events of Bloody Sunday.

CHECK THE FILM
The 1993 film *In the Name of the Father* is about the wrongful imprisonment of the 'Guildford Four' for an IRA bombing of a pub in Guildford in 1974. It depicts the police force's fabrication and suppression of evidence in order to convict four innocent people.

interpretation of the evidence. Like the other recorders, though, Lombard does remain emotionally detached from the dramatic events. In *The Freedom of the City*, Dr Dodds provides sociological commentary on poverty-stricken communities across the world, but cares little about the lives he describes. Lombard is similarly detached from O'Neill's plight. His manner is described as *'careful and exact'* (p. 6). He confirms Mabel's suspicion that he is more interested in Rome and the Counter-Reformation than matters of Irish nationalism. Whilst O'Neill and O'Donnell are hiding in the mountains, Lombard escapes to Rome.

There are discrepancies between Friel's presentation of Lombard, and the historical 'reality'. According to historical accounts, Lombard was certainly the Catholic propagandist that Mabel describes. However, O'Neill and Lombard did not meet until after the Flight of the Earls (1607), when O'Neill was exiled to Rome. In *Making History* Lombard intercedes between O'Neill and Spain. In history the Archbishop of Tuam was responsible for carrying the letters. Most importantly, Lombard's history, the *De Regno Hiberniae, Sanctorum Insula, Commentarius*, was a far cry from a *'Life and Times of Hugh O'Neill'* (p. 5). The *Commentarius* was an account of Ireland's history, which emphasised the country's role in the spread of Catholicism across Europe. It was distributed in 1600 to drum up support for the Catholic cause in Ireland from the Pope. O'Neill is presented as Catholicism's hope in Ireland. Because the *Commentarius* was written before Kinsale, the argument between Lombard and O'Neill regarding the representation of the battle (pp. 65–7) would have been irrelevant.

HARRY HOVEDEN

Harry Hoveden is Hugh O'Neill's private secretary. He is in his early forties, like O'Neill, and is described as a man *'who has a comforting and a soothing effect'* (p. 1). We know very little about Harry's background until the final scene of *Making History*. At this point, O'Neill explains that he 'chose one of the Old English' as personal secretary instead of 'a Gael', on the grounds that Harry might be above the 'petty venality' of 'small, tribal pressures' (p. 60). Harry, then, is not Gaelic, but a member of the Old English. The Old English came over to Ireland in the reign of Henry II, about one hundred years after the Norman conquest of 1066. Lombard refers to this in *Making History* when he argues that 'if we are to understand the Irish situation fully we must go back more than four hundred years – to that famous October 17 when Henry II of England landed here. He had in his hand a copy of Pope Adrian the Fourth's Bull, *Laudabiliter*, making him *Dominus Hiberniae*' (p. 12). The Old English settlers generally remained situated in the area in and around Dublin, called 'the Pale'. They pursued a less violently colonial course than their New English counterparts. By the Renaissance period, descendants of the Old English settlers were considered in a very different light to the New English 'upstarts'. The Old English were mostly Catholic. Although they felt they owed allegiance to the English crown, they refused to accept the Act of Supremacy, which made the English monarch head of the Protestant Church of England. The New English, however, were loyal to the monarch, politically and spiritually. The Old English suffered under a divided loyalty to the Catholic Church and to the English monarch. Harry may suffer from a divided loyalty in the same way that O'Neill is torn between loyalty to his clan and loyalty to Elizabeth I. In the final scene of *Making History*, O'Neill suggests that Harry's divided loyalty renders him a traitor: 'Don't you believe in loyalty any more, Harry?' he demands. 'In keeping faith? In fealty?' (p. 60).

Harry Hoveden is, in fact, very loyal to Hugh O'Neill. Their mutual dependence is exhibited in their speech patterns. In the first pages of *Making History*, O'Neill's speech consists almost entirely of **interrogatives** (questions). Harry's speech consists almost entirely of **declaratives** (statements), answering O'Neill's questions. ('O'NEILL: Yes? HARRY: O'Hagan's – where you were fostered' (p. 1)). O'Neill depends upon Harry to provide him with answers. When Harry does use interrogatives, it is with the purpose of encouraging O'Neill to speak further. For example, O'Neill wonders 'This jacket – what do you think, Harry? It's not a bit ... excessive, is it?' Harry responds 'excessive?' and O'Neill is encouraged to elaborate: 'You know ... a little too – too strident?' (p. 2). The verbal relationship between Harry and O'Neill contrasts markedly to Peter Lombard's **syntax**. Lombard poses **rhetorical** questions to himself, and answers them himself: 'I've come at a bad moment, have I? No? Good' (p. 60). Lombard's syntax doesn't

CONTEXT

Following the lead of her father, Henry VIII, in 1559, Elizabeth I reissued the Act of Supremacy which instated her as Supreme Governor of the Church of England. She also instituted an Oath of Supremacy, which required anyone taking public or church office to swear allegiance to the crown.

require the presence of another speaker. It illustrates his independence and egotism. Harry and O'Neill's mutual dependence is further illustrated by their use of identical phraseology. At first, Harry tells O'Neill the name of his flowers – 'Broom' (p. 1) – and he instructs him to 'give them plenty of water' (p. 2). When O'Neill returns on stage, he informs Harry that the flowers are called 'Spanish broom' and that 'they need plenty of water' (p. 3). O'Neill's imitation of Harry's information, and Harry's imitation of O'Neill's passive role, illustrates their co-dependence.

Brian Friel's Harry Hoveden is based on a historical figure called Henry Hoveden, or Hovenden. Henry Hoveden and his brother Richard were both foster brothers of Hugh O'Neill. Fostering was a common practice in Irish culture, in which children were brought up by another family. In the Renaissance period, Sir John Davies commented that this practice radically affected society: 'Fosterage has always been a stronger alliance than blood, and the Foster Children do love, and are beloved of their foster fathers ... more than their own parents and kindred'. In *Making History,* Harry's reminder to O'Neill that 'O'Hagan's place at Tullyhogue' was 'where you were fostered' (p. 1) is amusing in the light of this information.

Harry and O'Neill were historically fostered together. During the Spanish Armada of 1588, the historical Henry Hoveden was instrumental in capturing some of the Spaniards who found themselves in Donegal after being capsized by the English. At this point in history, Henry Hoveden allied himself to the crown. Later, he would become private secretary and friend to Hugh O'Neill, and assist the Spanish and Irish against the English. It is no wonder that in *Making History* O'Neill is unsure of Harry Hoveden's 'loyalty' (p. 60).

QUESTION

Is Lombard's version of history-writing a form of lying? How would you react to Seamus Deane's comment that 'the voice of power tells one kind of fiction – the lie ...The voice of powerlessness tells another kind – the illusion'?

THEMES

WRITING HISTORY

Making History is about history, and about how history is written. The true makers of history, Friel suggests, might not be the politicians, the monarchs, the rebels. The true makers of history might be instead the historians who change the way we perceive historical events. Friel had been interested in history-writing since he began his own writing career. In his first short story collection, *A Saucer of Larks*, the narrator of the story 'Among the Ruins' suggests that 'the past is a mirage – a soft illusion into which one steps in order to escape the present'. The representation of the past is bound up with memory. Human memory is fallible; we remember what we want to remember, in the way that suits us in the present. *Making History* suggests that historians alter the representation of the past to a similar extent as the human memory.

In *Making History*, the maker of historical events – Hugh O'Neill – is set side by side with the maker of his written history – Peter Lombard. We witness the clash. O'Neill wants to be represented honestly as 'the schemer, the leader, the liar, the statesman, the lecher, the patriot, the drunk, the soured, bitter émigré' (p. 63). Lombard wants to represent O'Neill as 'a national hero' (p. 67). This is a type of translation. The audiences of *Making History* witness the real person being translated into his historical image. In Lombard's history, the translated version clearly does not match the original. Friel is continually interested in the complicated matter of translation in his writing. He considers the issue most extensively in *Translations*, 1980, and *The Communication Cord*, 1983. Friel's chief source for *Making History* – Sean O'Faolain's *The Great O'Neill*, 1942 – described Lombard's representation of O'Neill as a type of translation. A play might be written, O'Faolain suggested, on 'the theme of the living man helplessly watching his translation into a star in the face of all the facts that had reduced him to poverty, exile, and defeat'.

Friel supports Lombard's view of history-writing, however painful it may be for O'Neill and subjects of biographical histories elsewhere. This is indicated by the fact that Friel exercises his own distortions of history in *Making History*. For Friel, real life and real people are too complicated and diverse to be represented by any single account. All histories are selective interpretations which, by inevitably leaving matter out, become types of falsification.

CONTEXT

The psychoanalyst Sigmund Freud profoundly affected the way in which people thought about human memory. Freud argued that there were two levels of the human mind – the conscious and the sub-conscious. Humans would often repress painful memories, would banish them from the conscious mind to the sub-conscious. Such memories would appear to be forgotten, but could continue to affect their owner through nightmares and nervous disorders.

CHECK THE BOOK

Friel's play *Molly Sweeney*, 1994, begins with a quotation from a poem by Emily Dickinson: 'Tell all the Truth but tell it slant'.

FACT AND FICTION

Is history-writing **objective**? Objective means the belief in a single, unalterable truth. Some sciences may be said to be objective. They believe in a reality which undeniably exists, and which their science seeks truthfully to represent. An objective historian would believe that, if enough research was done, it would be possible to uncover the single 'truth' of a past event. An objective historian would support O'Neill's plea for Lombard to tell 'the truth', to 'record the *whole* life' (p. 63). On the other hand, is history-writing **subjective**? Subjective means that every person's interpretation of reality is different. A subjective historian would not believe in one historical reality, in what 'really happened'. The subjective historian would consider, firstly, that every historical figure would have a different version of events. Secondly, the subjective historian would believe that historical evidence is interpretable in a number of ways. Peter Lombard is clearly a subjective historian, when he declares that 'I don't believe that a period of history – a given space of time – my life – your life – that it contains within it one "true" interpretation just waiting to be mined. But I do believe that it may contain within it several possible narratives' (p. 15).

Friel interprets the evidence regarding O'Neill's rebellion in his own way for *Making History*. He believes in the subjective right of the historian and playwright. Friel is extremely suspicious of any belief in objective fact. The scientists in his plays are given short shrift. In *The Home Place*, 2005, Dr Richard Gore believes that measuring the skulls and bodies of the rural Irish community will reveal the 'truth' about their identity. He uses science to support his prejudiced argument that the rural Irish are backward. In *Translations*, 1980, the Ordnance Surveyors seem to be innocently measuring the Irish landscape for a new map. In fact they are altering the landscape, anglicising its names, and imposing English rule upon it. Friel worries that the language of objective 'fact' and 'truth' is used to conceal a subjective, prejudiced agenda.

Friel supports the right of fiction to shape historical evidence into a narrative. This is not the same as a lie. The evidence is not ignored, but interpreted. It might be possible to accuse Friel of lying, or of just being wrong, when he positions the battle of Kinsale in 1583 in

Making History. But it might also be possible to argue that he distorts the dates in order to say something about the very nature of history-writing. *Making History*'s opposition of fact and fiction is also central to his play, *Molly Sweeney*, 1994. Molly is blind, but her husband Frank hopes the blindness may be reversible. Molly is subjected to science: 'Tests – tests – tests – tests – tests!' Science believes that the world of sight is the 'real' world. Molly is operated upon and becomes able to see. She is unable to interpret this new world of sight, and loses her grip on what is real and what is imagined. She lives in a 'borderline country' between fact and fiction. 'What I think I see may be fantasy or indeed what I take to be imagined may very well be real – what's Frank's term? – external reality. Real – imagined – fact – fiction – fantasy – reality.' Molly goes mad because the sighted community's notion of what is 'real' – i.e. sighted life – is imposed upon her. Instead, Friel argues, there are many different versions of reality, amongst which is the blind person's experience of life.

TREACHERY AND PIETY

In an interview with the BBC, Friel explained that he was attracted to O'Neill's 'capacity to dart into and out of his Gaelic consciousness and his English consciousness, his Gaelic experience and his English experience'. The division of loyalty between Irishness and Englishness defines O'Neill's character in *Making History*. As he explains to Mabel and to Mary, he is torn between loyalty to 'a way of life that my blood comprehends and indeed loves and is as old as the Book of Ruth' and loyalty to 'the new order which every aristocratic instinct in my body disdains but which my intelligence comprehends and indeed grudgingly respects' (p. 28). It is almost impossible for O'Neill to maintain loyalty to both sides without becoming a traitor. In his dual role as Gaelic chieftain of the O'Neill clan and Earl of Tyrone, he attempts this double loyalty. He is considered a traitor by both sides. Mary terms O'Neill to be 'a traitor … to the Queen, to her Deputy, to everything [Mabel] and I were brought up to believe in' (p. 25). O'Neill is officially proclaimed a traitor to the crown by the Lord Deputy, shortly before Kinsale (p. 36). O'Neill is also considered to have betrayed the Gaelic community. O'Donnell terms O'Neill's marriage to Mabel to be 'a class of treachery' (p. 14). Upon reciting

> **CONTEXT**
>
> Whilst also having connotations of spiritual devotion, 'piety' derives from the Latin word meaning 'duty' and it is this interpretation that occurs most frequently in Friel's writings. Lombard describes his history of O'Neill as 'an act of pietas' (p. 67) to the Irish nation.

his submission to the English crown, O'Neill predicts that his 'people' will 'crucify me for betraying them' (p. 50). O'Neill is caught in an impossible situation.

The theme of treachery dominates *Making History*. O'Donnell's frequent references to 'O'Doherty up in Inishowen' (p. 9) are veiled allusions to a historical figure who became popularly known as 'that audacious traitor'. O'Doherty was caught between English and Irish loyalties, too. He was eventually provoked into burning the city of Derry, of which he had just been made admiral by the English. He was executed by the crown. Ironically, in *Making History*, O'Doherty proves not to be a traitor to O'Neill. Whilst other Gaelic chieftains surrender to the Lord Deputy after Kinsale, O'Doherty continues 'holding out' (p. 45).

The opposite of treachery is loyalty. *Making History* is as concerned with fidelity as with betrayal. To whom should O'Neill be loyal? To whom is Mabel loyal? To whom is Harry loyal? To whom or to what should the playwright be loyal? O'Neill attempts to be loyal to two opposite camps, and is called a traitor by both. In the final scene, he sees himself in Harry Hoveden, the Old English private secretary who 'protested such fealty and faithfulness not only to Hugh O'Neill but to the whole Gaelic nation' (p. 60). O'Neill wonders if Harry's divided loyalty is a double betrayal: 'Don't you believe in loyalty any more, Harry? In keeping faith? In fealty?' (p. 60).

Mabel's loyalties are similarly hard to define. Her heritage is New English and she is able to 'calmly' criticise the Gaelic civilisation (p. 38). But Mabel is devoted to O'Neill, and O'Donnell recognises her as 'a loyal wee girl' (p. 48). The historical Mabel Bagenal left O'Neill shortly after their marriage to return to her English family. The words 'loyal' and 'loyalist' possess great meaning in Irish politics. A Loyalist is traditionally a supporter of the English crown. In *Making History*, however, the word can denote support of both English and Gaelic sides.

Making History presents a series of complex characters possessing divided loyalties. For Friel, multi-faceted identity was an inevitable aspect of humanity. The piety of the playwright, Friel explained in an interview, was to 'maintain fealty to yourself' (*Essays, Diaries,*

Interviews: 1964–1999, 1999), to represent the dividedness of the human condition.

PLANTATION

Queen Elizabeth I wanted to establish Ireland as an English colony. She achieved this through the confiscation of Irish land, and its bestowal on to New English settlers. In conversation with her sister, Mabel refers to the circumstances under which the Bagenals' Newry estate was obtained: 'I imagine the Cistercian monks in Newry didn't think our grandfather an agent of civilisation when he routed them out of their monastery and took it over as our home' (p. 24). This policy of confiscation was called 'plantation'. In the 1570s it was centred around the north-east Ulster region. English plantation provoked three rebellions, two of which were led by the Desmonds of Munster. These were suppressed. The Desmonds' lands were confiscated and given to English settlers. The third rebellion was O'Neill's.

This historical context illuminates the many images of planting and plantation in *Making History*. Mary tells Mabel about the Bagenals' literal plantation of their new estate. They have taken bog land and 'drained it and ploughed it and fenced it; and then planted a thousand trees in four separate areas' (p. 21). The Irish tended to practise pastoral farming, which involved using land as pasture for livestock. Mabel describes the 'millions of [cows] stretching away to the hills' (p. 16) on O'Neill's estate. The English considered this a waste and felt justified in their confiscation of land; Mary characterises pastoral farming as 'neglect of the land' (p. 24). The English preferred arable farming or 'husbandry', which involved the ploughing of land for crops. The planted English literally planted up Irish pasture. Mary attempts to persuade Mabel to adopt a similar policy on O'Neill's estate. She presents her with seeds for fennel, lovage, tarragon, dill, coriander and borage (p. 21).

The names of Mary's seeds are significant. O'Neill reads their meanings. Dill has 'a comforting and soothing effect', and he applies this description to Harry (p. 30). Similarly, the name of the Spanish broom, or 'genista', that O'Neill distributes around his room in the first scene is important. Its significance is described in **Extended Commentaries**, Text 1 – Act I scene 1 (pp. 1–4). The naming of

> **CONTEXT**
>
> Mary's view was supported by the English poet Edmund Spenser. In his *View of the State of Ireland*, 1633, he stated that 'if that countrey of Ireland ... be of so goodly and commodious a soyl ... I wonder that no course is taken for the turning thereof to good uses, and reducing that nation to better government and civility'. For Spenser, the Irish 'neglect' of the land justified English confiscation.

plants is an important ritual in Friel's plays. *Molly Sweeney*, 1994, begins with Molly's memory of her father teaching her the names, scent and feel of the plants in his garden. Friel is continually interested in how a person's name affects their identity, how place names affect the country, and the relationship between a word and the thing it describes.

DRAMATIC TECHNIQUES

DRAMATIC TIME AND HISTORICAL TIME

The stage directions at the beginning of each scene in *Making History* explain when the play is set. Act I scene 1 takes place in '*late August in 1591*' (p. 1), Act I scene 2 occurs after '*almost a year has passed*' in the summer of 1592 (p. 19), and Act II scene 1 is set '*about eight months later*' (p. 43), in the spring of 1593. The battle of Kinsale takes place between Acts I and II, somewhere between summer 1592 and spring 1593. The final scene of play takes place in Rome '*many years later*' (p. 54), after O'Neill has fled Ireland in the 1607 Flight of the Earls.

These dates distort the historical facts of O'Neill's rebellion. In the play, Mabel and O'Neill marry in August 1591, which is correct, but in history O'Neill and Lombard didn't meet until after O'Neill became resident in Rome in 1608. Kinsale happens between 1592 and 1593 in *Making History*, but in history the battle took place in 1601 (see **Characterisation: The historical figures and Friel's characters**). Friel's distortion of historical time for the purposes of dramatic time could be explained in a number of ways. The historical events of a decade are compressed into a couple of years. This allows for smoother continuity between scenes, and less physical change and ageing in the characters. Friel's distortion of time also has a thematic significance. His alteration of the date of Kinsale and the date of Mabel's death means that the audience is informed of both in the same scene. Mabel's death and Kinsale become related. Mabel represented hope for an amicable co-habitation of Irish and English communities in Ireland. Her death, and the death of that hope, occurs in the same scene that we hear about the defeat of O'Neill's rebellion and the English forces'

CHECK THE FILM

Friel's 1990 play *Dancing at Lughnasa* was made into a film by Sony Pictures in 1998. As part of this discussion of translation and distortion, it is interesting to consider how the film adapts Friel's script.

subsequent ravaging of the land. The domestic catastrophe is counterpointed by the political catastrophe. Friel's distortion of dates also indicates the diminished importance he places on historical 'fact'. *Making History* is a play about the **subjective** nature of history-writing. It suggests that every version of history is one possible interpretation out of many, and that no single history can represent the '*whole*' truth. It is debatable whether this 'whole' truth exists in the first place. Friel's conscious distortion of historical dates indicates his belief that every history is just an interpretation, and, to a certain extent, a distortion.

The seasons within which *Making History*'s scenes occur are important. The first scene occurs in '*late August*' (p. 1). In *The Achievement of Brian Friel*, 1992, Fintan O'Toole points out that *Dancing at Lughnasa* is set in late August too. This is a time of year in which summer is in 'full bloom but about to become overblown, the year [is] just about on the turn, time [is] ripening into decay'. August is a turning point for the worse, the time at which nature starts to wither and decay. The implication is that the prospects for Ireland and O'Neill will begin their downward spiral too. Act II scene 1 is set in spring 1593. Spring is traditionally a season of hope, of new beginnings, but this scene witnesses the death of all hope for O'Neill. He has been defeated at Kinsale, he will submit to the English authority which is ravaging his land, and Mabel has died. There is no hope in spring 1593.

PROPS AND SCENERY

Making History's stage directions are detailed regarding the play's props and scenery. At the start of the play, O'Neill's home is '*spacious and scantily furnished*' and his '*large living room*' is described as '*comfortless*' with '*no attempt at decoration*' (p. 1). This coincides with the description of O'Neill as a '*private*' man. The comfortlessness of his house reflects his inner loneliness. It is worth considering whether any character gets to know the 'private' O'Neill. The audience is given a glimpse of this private aspect when O'Neill remembers his education at the Sidneys' estate in England. Do Lombard, O'Donnell and Harry get to know this aspect of his character? Mabel draws close to the private O'Neill. This is reflected in the changed scenery of his house after almost a year of

CONTEXT

The watch referred to on p. 19 suggests that history can be made subject to the mathematical measuring system of time, that historical experience can be defined in terms of hours and minutes. Friel is sceptical regarding the use of scientific languages to represent human experience, particularly in *The Home Place* (2005). He is worried that science, which carries an aura of 'truth', often conceals a personal or political point of view.

marriage. The previously comfortless room has become '*more comfortable and more colourful*' (p. 19). In the final scene, however, long after Mabel's death and O'Neill's defeat at Kinsale, the scenery is described in identical terms to the first scene. It is again '*scantily furnished*' (p. 54) and similar furniture is present. In the first scene, O'Neill's room contained '*a large, refectory-type table; some chairs and stools; a sideboard*' (p. 1). In this final scene, there is '*a small table, some chairs, a stool, a couch*' (p. 54). O'Neill ends the play in similar isolation as he began it.

There are a number of other significant props in *Making History*. Lombard enters in Act I scene 1 carrying '*a large candelabra and an elegant birdcage*' (p. 6), gifts from the Pope (see **Characterisation: Hugh O'Neill and Sean O'Faolain**). In this scene, Lombard also holds copies of letters to and from Spain, and 'a résumé of my *Commentarius* – a thesis I'm doing on the Irish situation' (p. 7). In *Making History*, Lombard's *Commentarius* will become his history of O'Neill, and it holds a prominent place in the play. This prominence is indicated by its physical presence onstage. In the final scene, '*a large book – the history*' is placed '*in the centre*' of Lombard's desk, lit by '*the only light on stage*' (p. 54). O'Neill prowls around the book. He looks at it, '*his face close to it*', '*myopically he leans over it and reads*', and then '*he shuts the book in fury*' (pp. 55–6). The play ends with Lombard's '*public recital of* The History of Hugh O'Neill', but it takes place with the book itself shut and Lombard simply reciting '*by heart*' (p. 70). Like the 'truth' of history, and the 'privacy' of O'Neill, the actual content of Lombard's history remains inaccessible.

THEATRICAL MAGIC

In Friel's play *Crystal and Fox*, the ringmaster, Fox Melarkey, is a true showman. Through the power of words, he drums up audience excitement for his travelling show. To a degree, both characters represent the magical power of the playwright to create something out of nothing. Other plays are similarly interested in the magical and creative/deceptive capacity of words. In *Faith Healer*, 1980, Frank Hardy is a travelling faith healer whose verbal incantations induce his audience to believe he has cured their ills. Frank is the archetypal playwright. His words create an image of something out of nothing. In an interview, Friel compared theatrical magic to the type of seedy showmanship and deception described in *Crystal and Fox* and *Faith Healer*. 'I'm attracted to everything that's vulgar and cheap about theatre,' he explained, and compared himself to a 'conjuror'. 'It's a very easy thing to make [the audience] laugh … to make them cry[:] those are all very tempting tricks to play and they are cheap tricks and they are vulgar tricks.'

Successful playwrights and showmen can unite their audiences. Friel feels that 'to force an audience into a single receiving and perceptive unit is a very easy thing to do'. He is echoing W. B. Yeats' quotation of Victor Hugo, whilst working at Dublin's Abbey Theatre in the early twentieth century, that 'in the theatre the mob becomes a people'. The themes of unity and fragmentation are present in *Making History*. O'Neill tries, but is unable, to unify the 'fragmented and warring' Gaelic tribes of Ireland into 'a cohesive unit … a united people' (p. 11). Because of this failure his rebellion is defeated. O'Neill is not a successful showman. His words cannot convince his 'people' to believe in him like Frank Hardy induces faith in his audiences. O'Neill is not even unified in himself. He is riven by divided loyalties and perhaps, like Friel, finds it hard to believe in 'the wholeness, the integrity, of that Gaelic past' (diary entry for 15 May 1979).

THE POWER OF THE PLAYWRIGHT

The playwright has the magical power to make the audience believe in an illusion. The playwright has the power to change something into nothing, an empty space into a play. This power is not just limited to the theatre. Friel believes that drama has the power to effect political change. In *A Paler Shade of Green*, 1972, Friel suggested that 'one of our great misconceptions is that Ireland can be ruled only by its government and that the best government is composed of businessmen'. Instead, he argued that there was 'no reason why Ireland should not be ruled by its poets and dramatists'. With the actor Stephen Rea, in 1980 Friel founded the Field Day Theatre Company, which is described in more detail in the **Background** section. It was established to put politics back into Irish drama. Field Day emphasised the importance of touring theatre, of taking drama to rural populations and finding new,

CHECK THE BOOK

O'Neill is explicitly compared to a fox. In Act I scene 2 Hugh O'Neill remembers his childhood at the Sidneys' estate in England. He remembers Sir Henry's suggestion that 'those Irishmen who live like subjects play but as the fox which when you have him on a chain will seem tame; but if he ever gets loose, he will be wild again' (p. 35).

QUESTION

The quotation from Friel's diary suggests that Gaelic culture remains fragmentary for him. Do you feel this comes across in Friel's writing, and if so, how?

often working class, audiences. It sought to bridge political gulfs. In an interview in 1982, Friel felt that the Field Day project 'should lead to a cultural state, not a political state. And I think out of that cultural state, a possibility of a political state follows'.

Despite his description of theatre as 'vulgar and cheap', drama is a serious political matter for Friel. Theatre must be treated professionally. In a 1986 interview, Friel described his 'antipathy to amateur drama' and elsewhere he has argued for a systematic training of the actor, a professionalisation of theatre as a career. Theatre has the power to change politics, to make history. *Making History* traces writing's role in making history. In *The Diviner: The Art of Brian Friel*, 1999, Richard Pine comments that 'in *Making History* Friel makes the most serious claims yet for the authority of the playwright in describing the interaction of time and language, as the manipulator of "history"'.

LANGUAGE AND STYLE

Making History is mostly set in Ireland in the 1590s. The play features English and Irish characters. In the Renaissance period many legal, educational, and administrative interactions would have been conducted in Latin. The English characters – such as Mabel and Harry Hoveden – do not speak in sixteenth century English or Latin. They use the modern vernacular of the present era, complete with colloquialisms such as 'shut up!' (p. 20). This modernises the action of *Making History*, and makes the characters sympathetic for a modern audience.

Standard English is the model form of the English language currently taught in schools, as opposed to regional dialects. Mary and Mabel tend to speak in Standard English, although their speech is occasionally tinged with a Staffordshire dialect and '*a hint of Staffordshire*' in their accents. The Irish chieftains – O'Neill and O'Donnell – would historically have possessed a knowledge of Gaelic and Renaissance English. In *Making History* they use neither of these languages, but speak in Hiberno-English. Hiberno-English is the variety of English spoken in modern Ireland, in which Standard English has been altered by contact with the Gaelic language. Hugh O'Neill illustrates Hiberno-English when he says to Mabel, in his Tyrone accent, 'that's why you're fair dying about me' (p. 17). In history, Hugh O'Neill would have used English or Latin in official, court contexts, and Gaelic in communication with his clan. In *Making History*, O'Neill uses Standard English in his role as Earl of Tyrone, and Hiberno-English in his Gaelic persona. Mabel's speech changes over time to resemble Hiberno-English. This illustrates her growing sympathy with the Irish. Mary notes that 'you're beginning to talk like them, to think like them!' (p. 25).

Much of the characters' speech is realistic. Sentences are often broken off or interrupted, and this imitates real speech patterns. However, *Making History* is a literary work, and Friel controls the play's language so that it accords with the themes it describes. Through **metaphor**, a sentence may resonate on many levels. In Act I scene 2, O'Neill remembers Sir Henry Sidney's description of him as a 'fox'. The many different resonances of a fox – savage, primitive, sly, hunted and victimised – allow us to read this metaphor in a number of ways (see **Extended commentaries**, Text 2 – Act I scene 2 (pp. 34–5). Similarly, the play appears preoccupied with plants and flowers. They appear as props in the 'Spanish broom' (p. 2) O'Neill holds at the play's beginning, and the seeds Mary bestows on Mabel. On the surface, the plants are simply props. As a metaphor plants refer to the English colonisation of Ireland, a process called 'plantation'. The use of plantation imagery is discussed in the **Themes** section and the **Extended commentary** for the play's first pages. Friel is similarly sensitive to the way in which grammar may affect a sentence's meaning.

AND/OR

The words 'and' and 'or' are both **conjunctions**. 'And' expresses unity, the joining-up of elements. When Peter Lombard describes the need for the Gaelic tribes of Ireland to unite under O'Neill, he repeatedly employs the word 'and': 'And when I look at you what do I see? … a Gaelic domain, ruled by Gaelic chieftains. And how do they behave? Constantly at war … And how can fragmented and warring tribes be any use …?' (p. 11). Although he is describing political fragmentation, Lombard's use of the conjunction 'and'

? **QUESTION**

How far is the experience of reading *Making History* different from attending a live performance of the play?

creates syntactically the unity he wants politically. His **syntax** enacts his hopes for Ireland. Hugh O'Neill does the same when he describes to Mabel his task of trying to merge English and Irish interests: 'I have attempted to hold together a harassed and a confused people … And I have done that by acknowledging and indeed honouring the rituals and ceremonies and beliefs these people have practised … And at the same time I have tried to open these people to the strange new ways of Europe' (p. 40). The structure of the sentence supports its content.

Overwhelmingly, however, O'Neill's speech features the conjunction 'or'. To Mary he asks 'do I keep faith with … the Gaelic civilization …? Or do I march alongside the forces of Her Majesty?' (p. 27). 'Or' expresses a choice, and a division of elements. The critic Richard Pine has commented, 'if there is a controlling word in the whole language of *Making History* … it is: *or*'. He means that 'or' sums up O'Neill's dividedness, the conflict of between his Gaelic and Irish interests.

Making History is about the difference between 'and' and 'or'. 'And' represents the hope that the English and Irish can live amicably alongside one another. It represents the hope that O'Neill can unify the two communities, and the two aspects of his divided personality. Mabel – the personification of these hopes – predominantly uses 'and'. 'Or' implies that the English and Irish must remain separate, and that O'Neill must choose between them. He can support the English *or* the Irish, but not the English *and* the Irish. 'Or' represents the inevitability that O'Neill will prove a traitor to at least one community.

MUSIC

Many times in *Making History*, characters' speeches overlap, alternate, or occur at the same time. In Act II scene 1, O'Neill and O'Donnell alternate in reading O'Neill's submission to the crown. In the final scene of the play, O'Neill reads this submission at the same time as Lombard reads his history of O'Neill. In the play's first scene, O'Donnell describes the rotten floorboards at his house in Ballyshannon at the same time that Lombard and O'Neill discuss the correspondence from Spain. As described in the **Commentary** to Act I scene 1 (pp. 6–12), the overlapping of conflicting narratives

CHECK THE BOOK

A text's grammar can illuminate its content in fruitful ways. In *Shakespeare's Dramatic Language*, 1976, Madeleine Doran examines the use of the word 'if' in Othello. She suggests that Iago's use of 'if' demonstrates his faith in 'the world of … possibilities' and his belief in his own power to change reality.

is similar to a musical style popular in the period in which *Making History* is set, called 'polyphony'. Polyphony means 'many voices'. It featured multiple melodies occurring simultaneously. The music of J. S. Bach is a later, well-known, example. Polyphony is the perfect musical example of Friel's belief in multi-layered human personalities, as described in **Characterisation**.

Music is important to a number of Friel's plays. In *Dancing at Lughnasa*, Cole Porter's song 'Anything Goes', and traditional Gaelic *ceilidh* music, play whilst the women dance. In 'Seven Notes for a Festival Programme', 1999, Friel explains that the music functions as an emotional language in his plays. 'Music can provide in the theatre: another way of talking, a language without words. And because it is wordless it can hit straight and unmediated into the vein of deep emotion.'

There is no actual music in *Making History*, however. Instead, the sounds and structure of the speeches create their own musical aspect. The sound of the play's language possesses its own importance, alongside the meaning of its words. Friel's stage directions are almost as specific regarding the characters' accent, volume and articulation as a musical score. O'Neill is *'very angry, in Tyrone accent'* and then straight away he speaks *'quietly, in his usual accent'* (p. 14). Lombard talks with a *'careful and exact'* manner (p. 6). Mabel's *'accent has traces of Staffordshire'* (p. 15). Friel felt the language of a play resembled music, and he uses musical **metaphors** to describe the relationship between the playwright and the actor. The playwright's words, he suggests in 'Seven Notes for a Festival Programme', 'are scored in altogether different keys and in altogether different tempi' from the words of a novelist or poet. Great actors must be 'wonderful singers of the written line – perfect pitch, perfect rhythm'. Harmony in music and language can become a metaphor for social harmony; musical and linguistic disharmony can represent social tension. The jolting pauses and silences in Act II scene 1 contribute to the scene's image of a society falling apart.

CHECK THE BOOK
Music plays an important role in Friel's play, *Aristocrats*, 1980. Casimir's sister, Claire, is an accomplished pianist obsessed with Chopin.

PART FOUR

CRITICAL HISTORY

REACTIONS TO *TRANSLATIONS*

Making History partially grew out of reactions to Friel's 1980 play, *Translations*. *Translations* provided a picture of an early nineteenth century English project to make a map of Ireland, under the authority of the Ordnance Survey. In the process, as Friel describes it, Irish place names were anglicised; this reflected a wider imposition of English culture on to Ireland, in which aspects of traditional Irish culture were 'eroded'. In writing *Translations*, Friel did conduct extensive historical research. He read the real life Ordnance Surveyors' memoir of their Irish project alongside a modern historian's account. He read the letters of the Irish antiquarian and orthographer John O'Donovan – involved in the map-making project – and he researched the history of hedge-schools in Ireland, where the play is set. Despite this research, Friel chose not to reflect the historical facts accurately in the play. The actual director of the Ordnance Survey, Thomas Colby, was distorted into Captain Lancey, an authoritarian, violent personification of English imperialism. John O'Donovan, despite owning what Friel admits was an 'exemplary career', became in early drafts of the play a 'perfid[ious] quisling [traitor to his country]'. The dates of the mapping project were altered, and the surveyors were given greater military authority than they would really have possessed. Friel conducted these distortions consciously. In his diary entry for 22 May 1979, he considered what **genre** *Translations* fitted into. 'Inaccurate history?' Friel wondered.

Translations was generally received with overwhelming enthusiasm. However, some reviewers of *Translations* were quick to note, and criticise, the liberties Friel had taken with history. J. H. Andrews, the historian of the Ordnance Survey whose works Friel had read during his research, pointed out that mapmakers, even military mapmakers, would not have carried bayonets or exerted their authority on the rural population. Friel wrote a reply to Andrews in 1983, in which he sought 'to apologise to him for the tiny bruises

CHECK THE BOOK

Brian Friel has written the preface to the 2000 edition of John O'Donovan's *Ordnance Survey Letters Donegal.*

inflicted on history in the play'. Friel's alteration of historical facts in *Translations* remained a source of critical interest for many years after the play's first performance in 1980. In *The Achievement of Brian Friel*, the critic Sean Connolly complained that Friel's 'account of ... the Ordnance Survey is a hostile caricature'. Connolly pointed out that O'Donovan's involvement with the project was done in the spirit of Irish nationalism, rather than English colonialism. The recording of place names was part of an attempt to preserve ancient Irish culture and history. *Making History* can be seen as Friel's attempt to justify, in the face of these critical attacks, the playwright's right to provide a fictionalised account of history.

REACTIONS TO *MAKING HISTORY*

Making History provided reviewers and critics with a coherent argument by which they could understand Friel's approach to the representation of history, in that play and elsewhere. The programme notes for the first production of *Making History* explicitly stated Friel's prioritisation of fiction over historical fact. 'I have tried to be objective and faithful – after my artistic fashion – to the empirical method', Friel insisted. 'But when there was tension between historical "fact" and the imperative of the fiction, I'm glad to say I kept faith with the narrative.' Reviewers were excited by Friel's argument that every historical representation was simply one more interpretation, one more fictionalisation, of the facts. In the Irish *Sunday Independent*, Brian Brennan commented that 'Friel has presented us with a sort of dramatic Uncertainty Principal [sic] – the very act of observing and recording will alter the nature of the event or character so that the "reality" is lost forever'. Taking this idea of **subjective** history further, Brennan considered that every single performance of the play would create a different picture of O'Neill. It would be different every time, as there would be different audience members interpreting Friel's play in different ways. 'Each person who sees *Making History*,' Brennan mused, 'will, because of the nature of theatre, observe a different Hugh O'Neill begging to be portrayed as he *was*. And so, each member of each audience will be a party to the re-invention of Hugh O'Neill'.

QUESTION

Do you feel that a playwright owes a greater debt of responsibility to the 'facts' of history, or to the requirements of fiction? Can the two be compatible?

CONTEXT

The programme notes for the London production of *The Home Place*, 2005, noted that Brian Friel is 'particularly interested in the complex interaction, a mixture of both co-operation and conflict, between people and sometimes even within the one person or family, of different identities, educational influences, religions and nationalities, that is central to Ireland's history'.

Making History seemed to pacify the critics of *Translations*. Richard Pine, in *The Diviner: The Art of Brian Friel*, describes how, in the light of *Making History*'s argument regarding historiography, 'both John Andrews and Sean Connolly, the chief critics of *Translations* on grounds of historical accuracy, have revised their original objections and have come to accept the *bona fides* of the drama'. Sean Connolly did indeed accept the central argument of *Making History*, that 'historians commonly distort the past in order to serve the needs of the present'. However, Connolly finally observed in his essay that Friel's idea is 'undeniable, but also rather obvious'. Christopher Murray, in a chapter written for *The Crows Behind the Plough*, compared Friel's rewriting of history to the 'latest revisionist historical methodology'. Murray saw Friel's alteration of Hugh O'Neill's image as similar in intent to the historian Roy Foster's book *Modern Ireland 1600–1972*, which began 'with a re-assessment of the O'Neill legend'. Revisionist history is described more fully in **Historiographical background**.

Making History's critics responded positively to Friel's presentation of O'Neill's division of loyalties. In the programme notes for the 2005 London production of *Aristocrats*, Roy Foster commented, in relation to *Making History,* that 'Friel's view of history-making is as subversive as it is illuminating. In Ireland,' he continued, 'there are two truths, the Protestant truth and the Catholic truth' and we see the division personified in O'Neill. In *Making History*, Lombard had wanted to translate O'Neill into a nationalist hero for the Gaelic population of Renaissance Ireland to revere. Lombard's hero represented the strength and unity of Gaelic culture. Friel's O'Neill, however, has been read by critics as a representation, not of Renaissance Ireland, but of modern Ireland. Friel's O'Neill represents the deep psychic and real divisions of that nation. Foster sums this up: 'Friel's own importance in Irish life is far greater than that of chronicler or sounding-board. In plays of extraordinary subtlety, complexity and force he has interpreted a divided culture to itself.'

Friel's importance as a literary figure is demonstrated by the existence of around twenty-five critical studies of his works. These academic studies tend to examine Friel's importance to Irish theatrical history, and the relationship between Irish drama and

Irish politics. See **Further reading: Critical studies of Friel's plays** for a selection of references.

POST-COLONIALISM

One strand of contemporary criticism of particular significance for *Making History* is **post-colonialism**. Post-colonial literature is written in the wake of a history of colonialism. For the most part, it explores the effect of that history on the colonised country. Post-colonial criticism interprets post-colonial literature with a particular sensitivity to the relationship between the colonising and colonised nation. For example, Salman Rushdie's *Midnight's Children* creates an image of India's identity in the wake of a history of English colonisation. Post-colonial literature often finds that, after colonisation, even after the withdrawal of the colonising forces, the nation's identity is formed from a mixture of influences. The nation becomes a hybrid of the nation it once was, and the nation who colonised it.

In post-colonial literature the experience of the individual living in such post-colonial nations is often described in terms of homelessness and exile. The individual has lost the country they once knew and loved, and is alienated from the colonising culture. Such an individual feels like an outsider in their own nation. In a 1982 interview, Brian Friel described his sense that, in Ireland, 'you are an exile in your home in some kind of sense'. That Friel is interested in post-colonial theory is evident from his plays' emphasis on the figure of the homeless outsider, the exile. In *Making History*, O'Donnell states that 'those New English are all half tramps' (p. 14). At this early stage in the play, the colonisers are the outsiders. The play witnesses the reversal of this equation. The English make Ireland their 'home', and the Gaelic chieftains become homeless. In Act II, O'Donnell, O'Neill and Harry are literally homeless, hiding out in the Sperrin mountains and 'skulking about like tramps' (p. 44). By the end of the Act, O'Neill is literally exiled, to Rome.

Post-colonial citizens may feel exiled from their country's heritage, and from the culture of the colonising nation, but they may find a

CHECK THE BOOK
In 1980, Howard Brenton's *The Romans in Britain* was performed at the National Theatre in London. Brenton's play painted a brutal picture of imperialism in Ireland. It featured a scene of homosexual rape which became notorious, and provoked Mary Whitehouse to launch a private prosecution for 'procuring an act of gross indecency' against its director.

CHECK THE NET

www.cain.ulst.ac. uk is the website for CAIN, Conflict Archive on the Internet. It offers information and source material on Northern Irish politics from 1968 to the present.

new home in a culture that mixes elements of the two. A new hybrid society is offered in place of the two alternatives. The post-colonial critic Mikhail Epstein has described the location of this hybrid society at the 'crossroads of cultures' and Homi Bhabha has suggested that it constitutes a 'third space'. In *Making History*, Hugh O'Neill desperately wants to make this idea of a hybrid society a reality. As he explains to Mabel, he wants to allow Irish culture to mix with English culture. He attempts 'to hold together a harassed and a confused people by trying to keep them in touch with the life they knew before they were overrun … And at the same time I have tried to open these people to the strange new ways of Europe … to nudge them towards changing evaluations and beliefs'. It is almost impossible, O'Neill acknowledges, as these are 'two tasks that are almost self-cancelling' (p. 40). And, in *Making History*, O'Neill's task fails.

When the post-colonial third space fails to materialise in reality, it can be formed instead in the literature and language of the nation. Post-colonial literature often describes the hybrid that results from the cohabitation of colonising and colonised nations. Friel has suggested that his Field Day Theatre Company was 'a kind of an attempt to create a … province to which artistic and cultural loyalty can be offered'. Literature can offer a homeland when politics fail. The Field Day project, Friel hoped, 'should lead to a cultural state, not a political state. And I think out of that cultural state, a possibility of a political state follows. That is always the sequence' (interview with Fintan O' Toole, 1982).

PART FIVE

BACKGROUND

BRIAN FRIEL'S LIFE AND WORK

Brian Friel was born near Omagh, County Tyrone, in Northern Ireland, in January 1929. In an interview with the *Irish Press*, he explained that he has two birth certificates, 'one which says my birthday falls on January 9th, another which favours January 10th'. He was baptised Bernard Patrick Friel, an anglicised version of the name his parents really called him, Brian. The Friels were Catholic, living in a predominantly Protestant community, and may have felt that it was safer not to register him with a Gaelic name. Brian Friel, then, had two names, and two birthdays. 'Perhaps I'm twins,' he wondered. And perhaps his interest in divided loyalties and two-fold identities in *Making History* derives from this early childhood experience. Friel was brought up by his schoolteacher father and his civil servant mother. He had six aunts, two of whom moved to London before the Second World War, and died in poverty. Friel's play *Dancing at Lughnasa*, 1990, pays homage to this group of women.

When Friel was ten years old, the family moved to Derry, in Northern Ireland. In *A Paler Shade of Green*, he described the town as having 'two aspects ... one was of a gentle and, in those days, sleepy town; the other was of a frustrating and frustrated town in which the majority of people were disinherited'. Again, divided identity possessed interest, and pain, for Friel from an early age. The Friels were Catholic, and held in suspicion by the Protestant community. Brian Friel has recollected the everyday terror of his Derry upbringing. 'There were certain areas one didn't go into,' he remembered. 'I remember bringing shoes to the shoemaker's shop at the end of the street. This was a terrifying experience, because if the Protestant boys caught you in this kind of no-man's-land, they'd kill you ...That sort of thing leaves scars for the rest of one's life.' Friel's secondary education took place at St Columb's College, Derry, and when he was seventeen years old, he went south to study for the Catholic priesthood at Maynooth in County Kildare. It was evidently a traumatic time, and Friel rarely talks about it. In an

CHECK THE BOOK

In 2005, the Irish-born writer John Banville won the Booker Prize for his novel *The Sea*. *The Sea* describes the narrator's return to an Irish coastal town he visited as a child. It deals with the themes of memory and loss.

interview in 1990 he explained that it was 'an awful experience, it nearly drove me cracked. It is the one thing I want to forget'. Friel left Maynooth before being ordained and went to Belfast to train to be a teacher, like his father. He began teaching mathematics in Derry, and joined the nationalist party, but eventually 'resigned … because I felt the party had lost initiative'. In the 1950s Friel started writing short stories and was soon able to give up teaching altogether. He married Anne Morrison in 1954, and, upon starting a family, they moved to Muff, in County Donegal. Donegal is situated to the north-west of Northern Ireland, and is part of the Irish Republic but separated from it. Friel had positive early memories of Donegal. His mother had come from the region, and during childhood holidays the area had come to represent for Friel a form of imaginative and social freedom that he was unable to experience in Derry.

HIS WRITINGS

Brian Friel's career as a writer began whilst he was still a maths teacher in Derry. He began writing short stories, and in 1952 the *New Yorker* offered him a contract. His first volume of short stories, *A Saucer of Larks*, was published in 1962, and many of the issues that characterise his later plays are evident in these early writings. Between 1958 and 1962, Friel started writing radio plays. Two of these plays – *A Sort of Freedom* and *To This Hard House* – were performed on BBC Northern Ireland Home Service radio station. Friel was drawn to radio for its capacity to bring drama to communities, including rural working class communities, who might not have access to a theatre. One of the innovators of radio drama in the 1960s was Tyrone Guthrie, who like Friel derived from Ulster. In 1962, Friel went to visit Guthrie in Minneapolis, USA, where Guthrie was running a theatre company. Some critics consider that Guthrie 'kick-started Friel's theatre career'. Friel's first stage play to be professionally performed was *The Enemy Within*, which was staged at Dublin's Abbey Theatre in 1962.

Between the 1960s and the 1980s, Brian Friel was prolific. He wrote over twelve plays, which explored the way in which individuals' lives respond to their historical and political contexts. Themes such as divided identities and torn loyalties recur. In *Philadelphia, Here I*

CHECK THE BOOK

It is interesting to read *A Saucer of Larks* alongside *Making History*. From the beginning of his writing career, Friel has been interested in the power of memory to distort historical 'fact'. In 'The Fawn Pup', for instance, the narrator comments that 'memory is strange – and kind – in many ways. It will play back short, tantalizing sequences of the whole tape and then go silent'.

Come!, 1964, the protagonist Gar is represented onstage by two figures, Private Gar and Public Gar, to reflect two aspects of his personality. Gar is torn between affection and hatred for his Irish heritage, and desire and fear of the prospect of a future in the United States. During this period, Friel explored ways of representing these divided personalities and the subjective nature of reality. *Faith Healer*, 1979, consists of multiple monologues, each of which offers a different interpretation of events. The individual's psyche reflects the world in which it lives. The psyche is profoundly affected by politics, and political subjects dominate Friel's writing in this period. *Philadelphia, Here I Come!*, 1964, deals with Irish emigration, *The Freedom of the City*, 1973, angrily represents the shooting of civilians on Bloody Sunday, and *The Mundy Scheme*, 1969 – which Friel later retracted from publication – explores the nature of the Republic of Ireland's political independence.

Friel had never lost his earlier interest in making theatre accessible across a range of cultures. Initially he had managed this through radio, but by the 1970s he had become increasingly passionate about touring theatre. In 1973, the actor Stephen Rea played a part in Friel's *The Freedom of the City*, and came into contact with its writer. In 1979, Friel re-established his relationship with Rea and, in conversation, they discovered that, in Friel's words, 'we both wanted the same things and we decided to work together to achieve them'. They set up the Field Day Theatre Company, which would take professional drama to Protestant and Catholic communities in Northern Ireland and the Irish Republic. The first play produced by Field Day was Friel's *Translations*, which premiered at the Guildhall in Derry in September 1980. The criticisms of *Translations* for its historical inaccuracy have been mentioned in these Notes (see **Themes: Writing history**). Generally the play was enthusiastically received, and recognised for its importance. The *Irish Press* reported that its opening night was a 'unique occasion, with loyalists and nationalists, Unionists and SDLP, Northerners and Southerners laying aside their differences to join together in applauding a play by a fellow Derryman'. Friel did feel, however, that *Translations* was occasionally appropriated by political factions to which it did not belong. In 1983, he wrote *The Communication Cord*, a farcical counterpoint to *Translations*, to free the plays from such earnest

 CHECK THE NET

In 1980 Brian Friel and the actor Stephen Rea founded the Field Day Theatre Company. Extensive information about Rea can be found at **www.stephenrea. net**

CONTEXT

Friel frequently
expresses anxiety
regarding the
over-politicisation
of literature. In his
diary entries for
the days in which
he was composing
Translations, 1980,
Friel worried
about the
'political elements'
of the play. 'If it
becomes
overwhelmed by
that political
element, it is lost,'
he felt.

politicisation. *The Communication Cord* deals with the same issues of mistranslation and the erosion of Gaelic culture as *Translations*, but with hilarious comic effect. The first half of Friel's career as a playwright can be defined by its interest in historical drama. The plays explore the effect of history on the individual, and also how history might be represented onstage. These culminate in *Making History*, a cogent manifesto for the right of the playwright to fictionalise historical 'fact'.

In the latter period of Friel's career, he initially seemed to draw back from the historical context, to focus on the individual psyche. *Molly Sweeney*, 1994, describes the experience of a blind woman who learns to see again, and her subsequent descent into profound unhappiness and madness. *Dancing at Lughnasa*, 1990, narrates an aspect of Friel's personal history, and is based on the lives of his six aunts. However, in *The Home Place*, 2005, there is an evident return to his previous preoccupations. The play is set in the latter half of the nineteenth century, shortly before the advent of home rule. Like his earlier play *Aristocrats*, 1979, it explores the theme of the 'Big House' in Irish history. The English landlord, Christopher Gore, is neither at home in his estate in Donegal, nor at his English base in Kent. Gore is visited by his brother, who plans to use 'science' to demonstrate that the size and shape of the rural Irish population's skulls exhibit their tendency to dangerous and unruly behaviour. In *The Home Place*, Friel returns to a theme explored in *The Freedom of the City, Translations* and *Molly Sweeney* – the appropriation of the language of so-called fact to support arguments which are really based on dangerous prejudices.

Friel's achievement has been recognised and celebrated across theatrical, academic, political and civic communities. A theatre critic has commented that Friel is 'arguably Ireland's greatest-living playwright'. In 1987, the Republic of Ireland appointed Friel a senator in the Irish Senate, the upper house of government, where he served for two years. He has received honorary doctorates from five universities across Northern Ireland and the Republic. Friel is an honorary fellow of University College, Dublin, a member of the American Academy of Arts and Letters, and a fellow of the Royal Society of Literature. His plays are the subject of around twenty-five works of criticism. In 1989 the BBC marked his achievements in modern drama by putting on a six-play season of his works: Friel was the first living playwright to be honoured in such a way. His plays continue to attract enormous public interest; within a six-month period in 2005, four of Friel's plays were professionally performed to great acclaim in London.

HISTORICAL BACKGROUND

Historical context is crucially important to *Making History*. It is important to be acquainted with the historical period the play describes – the turn of the seventeenth century in Ireland – and the period in which the play was written – the late 1980s. The latter affects how the former is presented. This is the theory behind Lombard's explanation to O'Neill that the early seventeenth century 'isn't the time for a critical assessment of your "ploys" and your "disgraces" and your "betrayal" – that's the stuff of another history for another time. Now is the time for a hero' (p. 67).

HISTORY BEFORE *MAKING HISTORY*

The action of *Making History* extends over a period of twenty years, from 1591 to around 1611. The play refers to a lengthier history than that, however, and Lombard argues that 'if we are to understand the Irish situation fully we must go back more than four hundred years – to that famous October 17 when Henry II of England landed here. He had in his hand a copy of Pope Adrian the Fourth's Bull, *Laudabiliter*, making him *Dominus Hiberniae*' (p. 12). For the inhabitant of Renaissance Ireland, as for the inhabitant of modern Ireland, the present can only be understood in the context of a long history of invasion and colonisation.

The Gaels were a European branch of the Celts, and they arrived in Ireland long before the birth of Christ. By 500 BC, the Celtic culture and language was well established. The nation was divided into around one hundred small kingdoms, within five larger provinces. The whole was presided over by the High King, although it was often difficult to find one person who could unify such a sub-divided country. Around 500 AD, Christian influence began to spread across Ireland. This was aided by the fact that

CHECK THE BOOK

In *The Nature of History*, 1970, the historian Arthur Marwick explains that each age writes its own history, 'for each age will make a different evaluation of what is "significant" in its own past, will tend to see the past in the light of its own preoccupations and prejudices. History … is a dialogue between the present and the past'.

Christian missionaries brought with them the craft of writing. Ancient Gaelic stories began to be written down, and were tinged with Christian ideology. Despite its martial stereotype, this society was very stable. From the eighth to the tenth centuries Viking and Scandinavian invasions radically changed the face of Ireland, and walled cities such as Dublin and Cork were founded. In 1014, the Irish rebelled against Danish rule in the battle of Clontarf. After the battle, the Vikings remained integrated within the society, but the High King was killed, and the nation would never be unified again. In 1066, the Norman conquest of England took place, and a hundred years later the older Scandinavian power was replaced by the Anglo-Normans who began crossing over into Ireland. The first was Richard Fitzgilbert de Clare, known as 'Strongbow'. Back in England, Henry II worried that Strongbow might become too powerful in Ireland, so he appealed to Pope Adrian IV – the only English Pope in history – to grant him control instead. Adrian IV expressed Henry II's authority over Ireland in his *Laudabiliter*, meaning 'laudably', which made the English king, as Lombard describes, *'Dominus Hiberniae'*, King of Ireland (p. 12). In this period, English influence remained largely confined to an area around Dublin, called 'the Pale', and the English settlers generally became absorbed into Ireland. However, there were efforts to keep the English and Irish separate, and laws existed which made any interracial marriages punishable by death.

THE HISTORY OF *MAKING HISTORY*

The Tudor family came to the throne in England in 1485. In *About Friel*, 2003, Tony Coult describes this as 'a disaster for Anglo-Irish relations'. Ireland was a Catholic nation. The influence of Martin Luther had been sweeping across Europe for some time. Luther argued that the Catholic Church was rife with corruption, that salvation was a personal matter between the individual and God, and that the intervention of Catholic priests was unnecessary. In 1534, Henry VIII broke away from the Roman Catholic Church, and established himself as the Supreme Head of the Protestant Church of England. During the four years between 1536 and 1540, he disestablished Catholic monasteries across England, and sold two-thirds of the monasteries' land to the public. In 1547, when Henry VIII died, his Protestant son Edward – by Henry's third wife, Jane Seymour – acceded. Edward, however, died in 1553, and the throne passed to another of Henry VIII's children, his daughter by Catherine of Aragon, Mary. Mary had been brought up a devout Catholic, and she attempted to reinstate Catholic doctrines and rites in England. She was unpopular, however. Mary – who would become known as 'Bloody Mary' – martyred around three hundred Protestants. She also married the Catholic King Philip II of Spain, which provoked widespread xenophobia in England. When she died in 1558, she left no children. The only possible heir was Elizabeth, the moderate Protestant daughter of Henry VIII's second wife, Anne Boleyn. Elizabeth I set about undoing the work Mary had carried out in the name of Catholicism, and in 1559 a religious settlement restored the English monarch to the head of the Protestant Church. Elizabeth I's promotion of Protestantism became more extreme, and in 1563 an Act of Uniformity defined any defence of the Catholic Church as treason. Elizabeth's long reign, over forty-five years, united her previously fractured nation under one Protestant identity.

Ireland, as a Catholic nation, was treated differently by each member of this succession of monarchs, according to their religion. Henry VIII had assumed control over Ireland, in the name of converting the Catholic nation to Protestantism. He bribed his supporters in England and Ireland, by offering them land and titles. Henry's actions divided Ireland into three factions: the Old English, the Catholic Gaelic Irish and the New English. The Old English, who had come over to Ireland with the Anglo-Normans, were loyal to Henry VIII as king, but they refused to accept the role granted him by the Act of Supremacy, that of spiritual leader of the Church of England. The Catholic Gaelic Irish were opposed to Henry in both his roles. The New English, or 'Upstarts', whole-heartedly supported Henry, both as king and as head of the Church. They had profited from his bribes, and they shared his religion. Henry confiscated the land of the Gaelic chieftains, and returned it to them to regulate as landlords. This is an earlier version of the process O'Neill describes in *Making History*, of the English offer to the Gaelic chieftains of 'formal acknowledgement and recognition of what you already are – leader of your own people!' (p. 26). Henry placed a series of English Lord Deputies and Lord Justices to

> **CONTEXT**
> Mary I's marriage to Philip II of Spain was not a happy one. He was, by all accounts, a cold and indifferent husband; it was a marriage of strategy and political convenience.

preside over Ireland in his name. Even the Catholic Queen Mary I continued Henry's policy of 'plantation', the establishment of colonies of English and Scottish people in Ireland. The Protestant Elizabeth I's reign continued and accelerated the policy of plantation. It provoked three rebellions by Irish chieftains. Two, led by the Desmonds of Munster, failed. The third, led by O'Neill, is the subject of *Making History*.

? QUESTION

In *Making History*, Lombard articulates the view that 'because of [Elizabeth I's] mismanagement England has forfeited her right to domination over this country. The Irish chieftains have been forced to take up arms in defence of their religion. And because of your birth, education and personal attributes, you are the natural leader of that revolt' (p. 8). How far is this a biased viewpoint of O'Neill's motivations in leading the rebellion?

Hugh O'Neill possessed a dual allegiance. On the one hand, he was the Gaelic inheritor of authority over the O'Neill clan and the Country of Tyrone. On the other hand, as Mary describes it in *Making History*, 'Queen Elizabeth made you an Earl. And you accepted that title. And you know that that title carries with it certain duties and responsibilities' (p. 29). Before 1594, O'Neill had alternately fought on the side of the English and the Irish in conflicts. In 1594, he rejected his English allegiance, and rebelled against Elizabeth I's confiscation and plantation of Ulster lands. The Nine Years' War began in 1594 and lasted until 1603, when O'Neill was forced to offer his submission to the crown in the Treaty of Mellifont. During this Nine Years' War, England was in real danger of losing control of Ireland. At the battle of the Yellow Ford in 1598, the Gaelic forces defeated a four thousand-strong English army and killed, amongst others, the Queen's Marshal Henry Bagenal. The prospect of losing control over Ireland was terrifying to England. Catholic Spain had been in conflict with Protestant England since the Reformation, from the sixteenth century, and Ireland would be to Spain, as Lombard describes it, 'the ideal springboard for the Counter-Reformation' (p. 9). Henry VIII and Elizabeth I were particularly concerned about the prospect of Ireland facilitating a Catholic country's invasion of England. Elizabeth I adopted a ruthless military policy in Ireland. After the battle of Kinsale in 1601, the new Lord Deputy, Mountjoy, exacted cruel retribution upon the Irish people. O'Neill offered a submission to the crown's authority in 1603. It was not, as *Making History* implies, written whilst in hiding in the Sperrin mountains. When O'Neill was drafting the submission, he was unaware that Elizabeth I had died and had been succeeded by James VI of Scotland (James I of England). No one could predict the new king's policy regarding Ireland, and it has been suggested that information regarding Elizabeth's death was deliberately withheld from O'Neill. O'Neill was allowed to live, and was granted his title back, but, as he predicts in *Making History*, this constituted only 'nominal authority, without political or military power whatever' (p. 48). In 1607, devastated at this loss of power, a number of Gaelic chieftains and their entourages set sail from Ireland for the continent, where they would live in exile. From 1610 onwards, the plantation of Ulster with English settlers became unstoppable.

HISTORY AFTER *MAKING HISTORY*

England's plantation of northern Ireland in the seventeenth century sowed the seeds for political tensions that would last for centuries to come. *Making History* was written in the 1980s. It is a product of Ireland's present as much as its past. In the early twentieth century, political feelings were as strong as ever before. When the 1916 Easter Rising led to execution of many of its leaders by the British, nationalist feeling strengthened further, until, by 1919, Ireland was riven by civil war. In 1922, the south of Ireland became independent from Britain, and was termed the 'Irish Free State'. The Free State did not include most of the counties of the old province of Ulster. Here Protestants formed the majority of the population, and were fearful of a future amongst the southern Catholics. Most Protestants were Unionists (they supported the union of Ireland and Britain). Discrimination against Catholics became institutionalised to the extent that jobs, electoral power and housing rights were determined in favour of Protestant Unionists. A series of Civil Rights protests were organised by Catholic nationalists in the 1960s and 70s, who were assaulted by Protestant gangs and the police, and on Bloody Sunday in 1972 a number of protesters were shot dead by British troops.

The violence escalated towards the end of the 1960s, and the Unionist government sought aid from the British army. The Provisional Irish Republican Army (IRA), composed of a small number of Catholic nationalists, used violence against the army and police to try to overthrow the state. This, in turn, provoked violence from Loyalists. At the time in which *Making History* was written, heroes were created and evoked in support of political arguments. In *About Friel: The Playwright and the Work*, 2003, Tony Coult

CONTEXT

O'Neill's submission was known as the Treaty of Mellifont. It was written at the home of Sir Garret Moore, mentioned in *Making History*. Whilst hiding in the Sperrins, Harry informs O'Neill that Sir Garret 'wants to explore what areas of common interest might still exist between you and the crown' (p. 52).

explains that, in the 1980s, 'The greatest success (or disaster, for the British) of this period was the hunger strikes of the early 1980s, and in particular the death of Bobby Sands, a convicted IRA member ... his martyrdom focused Republican anger powerfully'.

Friel defines his sympathies as nationalist. *Making History*'s celebration of the Gaelic 'rituals and ceremonies and beliefs these people have practised since before history', in the face of 'the buccaneering, vulgar, material code of the new colonials' (p. 40), articulates a clearly nationalist viewpoint. However, *Making History*'s interest is in the possibility of reconciliation. In *Making History*'s final scene, set around 1611, O'Neill describes his journey down the 'Via della Conciliazione' (p. 54) in Rome. The Via della Conciliazione means the Road of Reconciliation. Its presence in *Making History* is **anachronistic** (see p. 52). The importance of the street's allusion clearly outweighs its anachronism. *Making History* interacts with the nationalist evocation of heroic figures that occurred in the 1980s. However, Friel's O'Neill is not heroic. Friel sets out to question the myth of Hugh O'Neill as a nationalist hero. He brings him back to human status. Instead, Friel creates a new kind of hero, a fallible hero in which two sympathies, two sensibilities, two nations reside at the same time. *Making History* can be read as a play of reconciliation, but whether that reconciliation can occur remains undecided.

Historiographical Background

The term 'history' is used to describe the past, and the study of the past. 'Historiography' is a word constructed from 'history' and 'graphology', history and writing. It is the study of the way in which histories are written. This is sometimes called 'metahistory', which means 'about history' or 'about history-writing'. When Hugh O'Neill and Peter Lombard discuss the historian's 'function' and 'method' (p. 8) they are taking part in a historiographical debate. O'Neill emphasises the importance of telling the truth, but Lombard suggests that history-writing should be a process of 'imposing a pattern on events that were mostly casual and haphazard and shaping them into a narrative that is logical and interesting', and he describes this as 'a kind of story-telling' (p. 8). Friel is dramatising a problem that besets all historians, whether to prioritise **primary sources**, or whether to tell a good story.

In 1838 the Public Records Office (now the National Archives in Kew, London) was established, and its equivalent in Dublin thirty years later. This made primary sources more accessible to historians. Histories of O'Neill could make more space for factual accuracy, or what O'Neill calls 'truth' (p. 8). Hiram Morgan's study, *Tyrone's Rebellion*, 1993, emphasises the importance of primary sources.

As *Making History* makes clear, however, histories of O'Neill have also consistently prioritised what Lombard calls 'story-telling' (p. 8). Story-telling is sometimes seen as working against the truth, as lying. Amongst the first historians of O'Neill was Philip O'Sullevan Beare, who included O'Neill's biography in his Latin history, *Historiae catholicae Iberniae compendium*, 1621, or, *The Complete Collection of the History of Catholic Ireland*. In 1687, James Ussher accused Beare of being 'as egregious a liar as any (I verily think) that this day breatheth in Christendom'.

It is important to ask why histories choose to tell stories. 'Story-telling' histories have often represented O'Neill as a Gaelic hero, fighting steadfastly against English oppression. Here, a myth can be more important than the 'truth'. The myth reinforces the Gaelic Irish's sense of identity and self-esteem in the face of English oppression. In *Making History*, Lombard is engaged in this patriotic task, and describes himself as offering to Gaelic Ireland 'Hugh O'Neill as a national hero. A hero and the story of a hero' (p. 67).

All history-writing is selective, a matter of choosing which sources are most reliable, and which events most important. The historian who aspires to academic 'accuracy' will try to select 'facts' that tell both sides of the story. Hugh O'Neill wants Lombard to write this type of history, when he asks him to 'record the *whole* life' (p. 63), and to make Mabel central. The mythical historian will select sources to confirm a story already present in the historian's own mind. Lombard describes himself as 'making a pattern' from the events of O'Neill's life, a pattern that forms 'a narrative that people will read and be satisfied by' (p. 67).

> **CONTEXT**
>
> In emphasising the importance of a woman who is invisible in published histories of O'Neill, Friel is engaging in a feminist historiographical debate. In *A Room of One's Own*, 1928, Virginia Woolf argued that history has tended to tell the story of famous men, and has ignored female achievements. She urges the need to tell these silent female stories, and, as an example, suggests that a history needs to be written of Shakespeare's (fictional) sister.

CONTEXT

Friel's play *Translations* shows a similar dependency on other texts to *Making History*. In *Translations*, Friel quotes directly from George Steiner's *After Babel*, 1975. It would be interesting to consider why Friel quotes so directly from his reading.

CHECK THE BOOK

The novelist Roddy Doyle depicts working-class Irish experience in his books. His 1987 novel *The Commitments* was made into a film in 1991. It portrays a young working-class man in Dublin as he forms a soul music band, and tackles themes of hope and despair.

Making History questions the validity of 'story-telling' historiography. In doing so, it alludes to a number of historical sources which support such a historiographical theory. The key texts mentioned in *Making History* are Peter Lombard's *De Regno Hiberniae, Sanctorum Insula, Commentarius*, 1600, Lughaidh O'Clery's *The Life of Hugh Roe O'Donnell*, 1603, and Sean O'Faolain's *The Great O'Neill*, 1942. All three histories distort 'reality' to create mythical heroes.

Peter Lombard's history of Hugh O'Neill was written around 1600, and was published in Latin in 1632, as *De Regno Hiberniae, Sanctorum Insula, Commentarius*, as he himself describes on p. 11. This can be translated as *Chronicler of the Kingdom of Ireland, the Island of the Saints*. Matthew J. Byrne has made a partial translation of Lombard's history into English, published as *The Irish War of Defence 1598–1600*, 1930. Lombard's book transforms Hugh O'Neill into a Gaelic hero in the way described by Brian Friel. He concentrates on O'Neill's military victories, rather than his defeats. This is because his book was written before Kinsale, as a propaganda tract. It was presented to the Pope in manuscript form in 1600, in the hope of drumming up support for O'Neill's rebellion.

In 1942, Sean O'Faolain published his biography of Hugh O'Neill, entitled *The Great O'Neill*. His book is the modern-day equivalent to Lombard's history of O'Neill, and Lughaidh O'Clery's celebratory *Life of Hugh Roe O'Donnell*, 1603. In his Preface, O'Faolain argues that, especially in narrations of O'Neill's life, historical accuracy should take a back seat to patriotic feeling. O'Faolain was a novelist, not a historian, and his book has been attacked by the rigorous historical scholar, Hiram Morgan, for its 'wild inaccuracy, crass romanticism and faulty revisionism' (*Tyrone's Rebellion*, 1993). *The Great O'Neill* was Friel's inspiration for *Making History*. O'Faolain begins his book with the suggestion that 'a talented dramatist might write an informative, entertaining, ironical play on the theme of the living man helplessly watching his translation into a star in the face of all the facts that had reduced him to poverty, exile and defeat' (p. vi). In *Making History*, Friel has clearly taken up O'Faolain's challenge.

REVISIONIST HISTORY

Revisionist historiography is defined by the *Oxford English Dictionary* as 'a revised attitude to some previously accepted political situation, doctrine or point of view'. Revisionism offers a counterbalance to accepted interpretations of historical events. A revisionist history of Hugh O'Neill would question the myth that has been constructed around the man. *Making History* can be understood as a form of revisionist history. It sets the myth of O'Neill as a 'national hero' (p. 67), against a different interpretation in which he is human and fallible. The critics Sean Connolly and Christopher Murray separately point out that Friel's play was written in the midst of a fashion for revisionist histories of Irish culture. Sean Connolly explains that, traditionally, Irish culture has been represented as having a history of poverty-stricken oppression at the hands of the brutal English. Revisionist historians have questioned the factual basis for this assumption. They have probed the British government's efforts to cope with 'the problems presented by Ireland, and at the real origins and character of a range of movements, like Hugh O'Neill's revolt in the 1590s, that were formerly accepted simply as so many episodes in a continuous struggle for national independence'. The critic Christopher Murray points out that Roy Foster's *Modern Ireland 1600–1972*, 1988, was published when *Making History* was first being performed, and that Foster's book begins with a revisionist reassessment of the mythologisation of O'Neill.

Revisionism can be understood in two ways. On the one hand, it attempts to make history-writing more professional. Revisionist histories question myths and re-examine available evidence. They don't accept a single interpretation of history, but suggest that historical experience is **subjective**. Revisionism is also very political. Revisionism often chooses to question historical interpretations which support the oppressed. For example, revisionist historians might suggest that, contrary to the accepted view, the Holocaust did not occur, or its effects were not as devastating as previously thought. Revisionist historians might argue that there were as many white slaves as black slaves. In this context, revisionist history supports a conservative point of view. It argues against 'political correctness', and denies the responsibility of the historical

QUESTION

Do you feel that Friel's deconstruction of the myth of O'Neill sets out to undermine Irish nationalist politics? What might be his other motives for re-writing O'Neill's story?

oppressor. In the context of *Making History*, the revisionist deconstruction of the myth of O'Neill as a 'national hero' might be understood as an attempt to undermine Irish nationalism by removing one of its historical sources of pride. It is important to be attuned to this political dimension of historical practice.

LITERARY BACKGROUND

IRISH THEATRE

How does one define Irish theatre? In his essay 'Plays Peasant and Unpeasant', Friel defines Irish drama as 'plays written in Irish or English on Irish subjects and performed by Irishmen'. This is not as obvious a definition as it might seem. Before the twentieth century, Irish literature *had* been absorbed into the canon of 'great' literature in English. However, the most well-known of Irish writers tended to write in English, on English subjects, and their plays were performed by English actors. Brian Friel suggests that modern Irish drama, as he defines it, began on 8 May 1899, at the premiere of William Butler Yeats' play *Countess Cathleen*. This was followed by *Cathleen ni Houlihan*, a play based on ancient Irish texts which personified Ireland as the woman Cathleen. In *Making History*, O'Donnell refers to the female personification of the Irish nation when he declares that 'the land is the goddess that every ruler in turn is married to' (p. 47). Yeats established drama as a forum for discussions regarding Irish identity. He founded the Irish National Theatre Society, which was based at the Abbey Theatre in Dublin, but was also committed to touring. The first two decades of the twentieth century was an exciting time for Irish drama. The playwright J. M. Synge, author of *The Playboy of the Western World*, 1907, was discovered. Friel has defined Synge as 'the man who made Irish theatre'. By the mid-twentieth century, however, the Abbey had become less politicised in Friel's view. It tended to look towards the rural centre of Ireland, whilst another Dublin theatre, the Gate, looked towards Europe for innovations in staging, lighting and play-writing.

THE FIELD DAY THEATRE COMPANY

Brian Friel's writing career began with short stories and radio plays.

CONTEXT

The 'canon' is the term used to refer that set of authors generally considered to be 'great', to possess 'genius', to be worthy of being studied in schools and universities. How writers become canonical is a thorny issue. The critic Harold Bloom argues that it is down to innate 'genius'. Generally, however, the current thinking is that authors are accepted into the canon who conform to the prejudices and preferences of society. Hence, until recently most of the literature taught in schools was written by white men.

He was drawn to radio's capacity to bring drama to communities who might otherwise be denied access to theatre. This interest stayed with him and, in the 1970s he became increasingly passionate about touring theatre. In 1973, the actor Stephen Rea played a part in Friel's *The Freedom of the City*, and came into contact with its writer. In 1979, Friel re-established his relationship with Rea and they discovered that, in Friel's words, 'we both wanted the same things and we decided to work together to achieve them'. They founded a theatre company, partly to raise funding for the production of Friel's play *Translations*, but mostly to fulfil their hopes of unifying Ireland through drama. The company was called the Field Day Theatre Company, a name which sounded like the two men's names – Friel/Field, Rea/Day – and connotations of the military, the landscape, hunting, and joy and triumph, having a 'field day'.

Translations proved an enormous success. It was felt by Friel and Rea that Field Day could continue beyond *Translations*, and become something more than a theatre company. It seemed that it offered an opportunity for the exploration of different histories and cultural identities within Northern Irish politics. The poet Seamus Heaney wholeheartedly encouraged the exercise, and wanted Friel to 'keep the energy rolling because my sense of that moment and that play was that this was what theatre was supposed to do'. The Board of Field Day was enlarged to include four more directors: Heaney, the poet and literary critic Tom Paulin, the writer Seamus Deane and David Hammond, a broadcaster and musician. Three were Protestants, three were Catholics. It was felt, by Paulin in particular, that Field Day allowed its members to transcend the difficult divisions of modern Ireland. Alongside the traditional four provinces of Ireland – Munster, Leinster, Connaught and Ulster – Field Day formed 'a fifth province to which artistic and cultural loyalty can be offered'. Irish literature offered a homeland in compensation for the difficulties of the real homeland. In an interview in 1982, Brian Friel described how 'Field Day has grown out of that sense of impermanence, of people who feel themselves native to a province or certainly to an island but in some way feel that a disinheritance is offered to them'. It is no coincidence that Field Day was based in Derry. Derry is a city on the border of

CHECK THE NET

www. fielddaybooks. com describes the publications of the Field Day Theatre Company, established in 1980 by Brian Friel and Stephen Rea.

CONTEXT

By the 1960s, Derry was badly in need of a new university to accommodate the numbers of educated Catholics. However, the Northern Irish government decided to establish the new university in the small, Unionist town of Coleraine instead. Field Day's presence in Derry might be seen as an attempt to rectify the city's history of academic deprivation.

Northern Ireland and the Republic, a divided city where Friel grew up and whose divisions were emblematic of those Field Day sought to heal.

Field Day engaged in numerous cultural activities. Throughout the 1980s and 1990s it produced new plays and new translations. In 1983, Field Day oversaw the publication of pamphlets dealing with issues relevant to modern Ireland, including language, colonialism and Anglo-Irish senses of identity. It also published a five volume anthology of Irish literature, from ancient times to the present. It instigated a series of academic texts considering Irish culture, history and literature. Friel resigned from Field Day in 1994, feeling that it had become too beset by politics. He had articulated his frustration at the intrusion of politics into literature at the beginning of the Field Day project, when he protested that *Translations* had been offered political 'pieties that I didn't intend for it'. Friel emphasises the importance of developing a writer's voice which is separate from political sympathies. 'I think the moment you begin huckstering in the public domain and huckstering with the public language, and with the public political discourse, then you are in danger because you are endangering the discourse with oneself,' he stated in an interview in 1986.

CHECK THE BOOK

Hollywood Irish: In Their Own Words, 1997, is an illustrated collection of interviews with Irish actors such as Liam Neeson, Pierce Brosnan, and Stephen Rea, who co-founded the Field Day Theatre Company with Friel. The interviews consider the importance of Irish identity to the actors' lives.

THOMAS KILROY'S *THE O'NEILL* (1962)

In 1986, Field Day produced Thomas Kilroy's *The Double Cross*, which Friel praised for its ability to unify the audience 'into a single receiving and perceptive unit'. Kilroy joined Field Day's board of directors in 1988. He was the only member from the Irish Republic. Kilroy had written a play based on Hugh O'Neill prior to becoming associated with Field Day, in 1962. Friel would certainly have read Kilroy's version of the history he would adapt for *Making History*.

Brian Friel's *Making History* shares some important similarities with Thomas Kilroy's *The O'Neill*. Both plays are structured around a battle which occurs in the middle, but which happens offstage. *Making History* is centred around the Irish defeat at Kinsale. *The O'Neill* revolves around the Irish victory at the battle of the Yellow Ford in 1598, but ends with the defeat at Kinsale and O'Neill's submission to Elizabeth I. Both plays are preoccupied with Mabel Bagenal's role in O'Neill's rebellion. In *Making History*, she represents the possibility of Anglo-Irish cohabitation. In *The O'Neill*, she represents the adoption of English culture by the Gaelic chieftains which, in the play, fails. She leaves O'Neill and returns to her family, as it appears she did in history. Hugh O'Neill is represented by both Friel and Kilroy as a divided figure, torn between loyalty to the English and loyalty to his tribe, and in possession of different public and private personas. 'Only half of myself belongs to myself – the other half belongs to the people,' Kilroy's O'Neill ruefully comments, and in the same play Mabel complains that 'You're one thing to one man and something else to another. It's like being a living lie.'

The O'Neill of *Making History* is a more human and sympathetic character than Kilroy's O'Neill. The latter mistreats Mabel, cares little when she leaves him, and is a volatile and egotistical leader who seeks personal aggrandisement as 'king of all Ireland'. Both plays use hunting **metaphors** to describe the English crown's pursuance of O'Neill. In *Making History*, the English Sir Henry Sidney describes O'Neill as 'Fox O'Neill' who is 'as the fox which when you have him on a chain will seem tame; but if he ever gets loose, he will be wild again' (p. 35). In *The O'Neill*, O'Neill is described by Elizabeth I as 'her Great Running Beast'. After Kinsale, he comments that 'The hunt is over. She can draw off her hounds. Silence her hunting horns.' The final scenes of *Making History* and *The O'Neill* are strikingly similar. Both end with a recitation of O'Neill's submission to the crown, and, in both cases, this submission derives from the historical document of 'The Humble Submission Of The Earl Of Tyrone Before The Lord Deputy And Council, At Dublin, The 8th April Of 1603'. Friel's version of O'Neill's history is far more nuanced and complex than Kilroy's. It considers the mythologisation of O'Neill's character, and the nature of historiography.

CHECK THE BOOK

Friel's play *Crystal and Fox*, 1970, also uses these hunting metaphors. The protagonist is called Fox Melarkey. He repeatedly sings the refrain 'A-hunting you will go,/ You'll catch no fox and put him in a box,/ 'A-hunting you will go'.

GEOGRAPHICAL BACKGROUND

Geography and land is crucial to *Making History*. The history of Anglo-Irish tension revolves around the question of who inhabits what land (see **Historical background: History before *Making History***). Geography was crucially important to the military tactics of O'Neill's rebellion. O'Neill and O'Donnell were powerful in the north of Ireland, in Ulster, where they were most likely to rally soldiers and support. The Spanish, however, landed at Kinsale, in the south of Ireland. Between the two, the English established, as O'Donnell describes, 'a line of forts right across the country from Dundalk over to Sligo' (p. 9). The Spanish fleet's decision to land at Kinsale meant that O'Neill and O'Donnell had to march their troops the length of Ireland to meet them, across a line of English fortifications. When they finally arrived, exhausted, in the south, the presence of English soldiers prevented them from meeting the Spanish troops. It was impossible for the Irish and Spanish to discuss the tactics, timing or co-ordination of an assault upon the English. When the battle of Kinsale started, such disorganisation meant that an English victory was inevitable. In *Making History*, O'Donnell repeatedly demonstrates wilful geographical ignorance. When Lombard explains that the Spanish are planning on landing in Kinsale, he declares he's 'never heard of it' (p. 32). 'Wherever that is' becomes O'Donnell's mantra (p. 32). O'Neill is acutely conscious of the importance of geography to his rebellion. He is aware that 'Kinsale is out of the question. If they insist on landing in the south – anywhere in the south – tell them to cancel the expedition' (p. 35). Unfortunately, his commands are ignored.

CHECK THE BOOK

Ruth Dudley Edwards' *Atlas of Irish History*, 1973, illustrates the geographical changes that have affected Ireland on a series of maps.

Flight of the Earls to Rome

ATLANTIC OCEAN

Derry

SPERRIN MTNS.

1.

ULSTER

2.

Tullyhogue

Dungannon

Sligo

Newry

Dundalk

CONNAUGHT

Mellifont Abbey

The Pale

LEINSTER

Dublin

MUNSTER

Kinsale

Spanish fleet lands

1. *Tyrconnell*
(O'Donnell's jurisdiction)

2. *County Tyrone*
(O'Neill's jurisdiction)

Events in Ireland and England	Author's life	Literary Events
c. 1500 The Renaissance comes to Northern Europe		
1509 Henry VIII ascends to the English throne		
1534 Henry VIII is confirmed as 'Supreme Head of the Church of England'. England officially breaks with the Roman Catholic Church		
1536–40 Henry VIII dissolves England's monasteries		
1541 Irish parliament recognises Henry VIII as 'King of Ireland'		
1547 Edward VI becomes King of England at 9 years old		
1550 Birth of Hugh O'Neill		
1553 Mary I becomes Queen of England, and marries the Catholic King Philip II of Spain		
c. 1555 Birth of Peter Lombard		
1556 Birth of Henry Bagenal		
1558 Elizabeth I becomes Queen, and England becomes Protestant again		
1563 Birth of Charles Blount, Lord Mountjoy		
1571 Birth of Hugh Roe O'Donnell		
		c. 1581 Philip Sidney, *A Defence of Poesy*
1587 Hugh Roe O'Donnell kidnapped by Lord Deputy		
1588 Spanish Armada		
1590 Lord Deputy hangs Hugh Roe MacMahon, rebel against plantation in Ulster		**1590** Edmund Spenser, *The Faerie Queene* (part one); first recorded London performance of Shakespeare's plays

Events in Ireland and England	Author's life	Literary Events
1591 Mabel (christened Ursula) Bagenal and Hugh O'Neill marry		
1592 O'Donnell escapes from English captivity, and becomes leader of O'Donnell clan		
1593 Hugh O'Neill inaugurated as The O'Neill		
1594 Nine Years' War begins		
1595 O'Neill destroys Blackwater Fort		
1595 Mabel O'Neill, née Bagenal, dies		
		1596 Edmund Spenser begins *View of the State of Ireland*
1598 Battle of the Yellow Ford; death of Henry Bagenal		
1600 Pope Clement VIII provides O'Neill with a Bull of Indulgence		**1600** Lombard gives manuscript of *De Regno Hiberniae, Sanctorum Insula, Commentarius* to Pope Clement VIII
1601 Lombard is made Archbishop of Armagh, whilst living in Rome		
1601 Earl of Essex, Robert Devereux, executed for treason		
1601 Defeat of Spanish and Gaelic armies at battle of Kinsale		
1602 Hugh O'Donnell dies in Spain, possibly poisoned		
1603 End of Nine Years' War; O'Neill submits to English authority in Treaty of Mellifont; beginning of Plantation of Ulster; Elizabeth I dies and James I of England (James VI of Scotland) ascends to throne		**1603** Lughaidh O'Clery, *The Life of Hugh Roe O'Donnell*
		1605 first version of Shakespeare's *King Lear*

Events in Ireland and England	Author's life	Literary Events
1606 Death of Charles Blount, Lord Mountjoy		
1607 Flight of the Earls		
1607–9 O'Doherty's rebellion		
1608 O'Neill arrives in Rome		
1609 Mary Barnewall, née Bagenal, dies		
1610 The Printed Book, publication of James I's plan of Plantation		
1616 Hugh O'Neill dies in Rome		
		1616 William Shakespeare dies
1625 Lombard dies in Rome; Charles I replaces James I		
		1633 John Donne, *Collected Poems* published posthumously
1641 Great Catholic–Gaelic Rebellion		
1649 Cromwell arrives in Ireland; Charles I executed		
1650 Catholic landowners in Ulster exiled		**1650** Andrew Marvell, 'An Horatian Ode upon Cromwell's Return from Ireland'
1660 Monarchy restored and Charles II becomes king		
		1667 John Milton, *Paradise Lost*
1685 Catholic King James II ascends to throne		
1688–9 105-day siege of Derry. Mountjoy's garrison is besieged by a Catholic regiment		
1689 William of Orange (Protestant) defeats James II at battle of the Boyne		

Events in Ireland and England	Author's life	Literary Events
		1690–1780 High point of Gaelic aisling, or 'vision', poetry
1695 First penal laws exacted against Catholics		
		1709 George Berkeley, *An Essay Towards a New Theory of Vision*
		1725 Jonathan Swift, *Gulliver's Travels*
1775 Birth of Daniel O'Connell, campaigner for Catholic emancipation		
1789 French Revolution		
		1790 Edmund Burke, *Reflections on the Revolution in France*
1791 Ordnance Survey officially constituted in England		
1798 United Irishmen rebel		
		1800 Maria Edgeworth, *Castle Rackrent*
1801 Act of Union between England and Ireland comes into force		
		1814 Jane Austen, *Mansfield Park*
1816–42 Devastating famines due to potato blight		
1823 O'Connell forms Catholic Association		
1824 Ordnance Survey begins work in Ireland		
1829 Catholic Emancipation Act (Catholics are allowed to become MPs)		**1829** William Wordsworth tours Ireland, and writes 'not a single poem' based on his experiences
1831 Founding of National Schools		
1841 Irish population at 8 million		

Events in Ireland and England	Author's life	Literary Events
1845–9 Great Famine. 1 million people die, 1.5 million emigrate		
		1852 Birth of one of the leading figures of the Irish Revival, Lady Augusta Gregory
		1856 George Bernard Shaw born
1858 Founding of Irish Republican Brotherhood; in America, founding of Fenian Brotherhood		
		1865 Samuel Ferguson, *Lays of Western Gael*
1886 First Home Rule Bill is not passed in Parliament		
1893 Second Home Rule Bill is also rejected by Parliament		
		1902 W. B. Yeats, *Cathleen Ni Houlihan*
		1904 George Bernard Shaw, *John Bull's Other Island*
		1907 J. M. Synge, *Playboy of the Western World*
1912 Third Home Rule Bill		
1914–18 First World War		**1914** James Joyce, *Dubliners*
1916 Easter Rising		
1920 Southern and Northern Ireland partitioned		
		1922 James Joyce, *Ulysses*
		1924 Sean O'Casey, *Juno and the Paycock*
	1929 Brian Friel born near Co. Tyrone in Northern Ireland	

Events in Ireland and England	Author's life	Literary Events
1939 IRA bombing campaign in Britain	**1939** Friel family move to Derry	
1939–45 Second World War		
	1941–6 Friel's secondary education at St Columb's College, Derry	
		1942 Patrick Kavanagh, *The Great Hunger*; Sean O'Faolain, *The Great O'Neill*
	1946–8 Friel studies for priesthood at St Patrick's College, Maynooth, but leaves before ordination	
1949 Declaration of Republic of Ireland bill	**1949** Friel trains as a teacher in Belfast	
	1950 Friel teaches maths in Derry schools	
	1952 Friel offered short story writing contract by *New Yorker*	
	1954 Brian Friel and Anne Morrison marry; family later move to Muff, Co. Donegal	
		1955 Samuel Beckett, *Waiting for Godot*
1956–62 IRA campaign in the north of Ireland		
	1958–62 Friel's radio plays *A Sort of Freedom* and *To This Hard House* are aired on BBC	**1958** Brendan Behan, *The Hostage*
	1960 *A Doubtful Paradise* produced in Belfast. Friel gives up teaching to write	
		1961 Thomas Murphy, *A Whistle in the Dark*
	1962 Short story collection *A Saucer of Larks* published. Play, *The Enemy Within*, staged at Abbey Theatre, Dublin. Friel visits Tyrone Guthrie in USA	**1962** Thomas Kilroy, *The O'Neill*

Events in Ireland and England	Author's life	Literary Events
	1964 *Philadelphia, Here I Come!* staged	
	1966 A second volume of short stories, *The Gold in the Sea*, published. *The Loves of Cass McGuire* staged	**1966** John B. Keane, *The Field*
	1967 *Lovers* staged	
1968 First Civil Rights March	**1968** *Crystal and Fox* staged	
1969 Sectarian violence breaks out in Northern Ireland	**1969** *The Munday Scheme* staged, and later withdrawn	
	1971 *The Gentle Island* staged	
1972 'Bloody Sunday' takes place in Derry		
	1973 *The Freedom of the City*, based on Bloody Sunday, is staged	**1973** Paul Muldoon, *New Weather*
	1975 *Volunteers* staged	**1975** Seamus Heaney, *North*
	1977 *Living Quarters* staged	
	1979 *Faith Healer* staged in New York; *Aristocrats* staged in Dublin	
1980 Ten IRA hunger strikers die; riots in Northern Ireland	**1980** Brian Friel and Stephen Rea found Field Day; *Translations* is its first production	**1980** Howard Brenton, *The Romans in Britain*
	1981 Adaptation of Chekhov's *Three Sisters* staged	
		1983 Tom Paulin, *The Liberty Tree*
1985 Anglo-Irish Agreement		**1985** Frank McGuinness, *Observe the Sons of Ulster Marching Towards the Somme*
		1986 Thomas Kilroy, *Double Cross*
	1987 Adaptation of Turgenev, *Fathers and Sons* staged; Friel appointed to Irish senate	
	1988 *Making History* staged	

Events in Ireland and England	Author's life	Literary Events
	1990 *Dancing at Lughnasa* staged	
	1992 Adaptation of Charles Macklin's *The True Born Irishman*, under the title *The London Vertigo*; adaptation of Turgenev's *A Month in the Country*	**1992** Frank McGuinness, *Someone Who'll Watch Over Me*
1993 Beginning of Northern Ireland Peace Process	**1993** *Wonderful Tennessee* staged	
	1994 *Molly Sweeney* staged; Friel leaves Field Day	**1994** Marina Carr, *The Mai*
		1996 Martin McDonagh, *The Beauty Queen of Leenane*
	1997 *Give Me Your Answer, Do!* Staged	**1997** Conor McPherson, *The Weir*
1998 Good Friday Agreement; Tony Blair commissions Saville Inquiry to reappraise Bloody Sunday	**1998** Adaptation of Chekhov's *Uncle Vanya* staged; film version of *Dancing at Lughnasa* released	
1999 New Devolved Government formed in Northern Ireland		
2000 Devolved assembly briefly suspended when IRA refuses to commit to decommissioning of its weapons		
	2002 *Three Plays After*, versions of Chekhov's writings, staged	
	2003 *Performances* staged	
2005 IRA declares its armed campaign is over, confirms its weapons have been taken out action, and promises to pursue aims through politics	**2005** *The Home Place* staged	
2006 Results of Saville Inquiry		

OTHER WORKS BY BRIAN FRIEL

Brian Friel: Essays, Diaries, Interviews 1964–1999, Faber and Faber, 1999

Brian Friel in Conversation, University of Michigan Press, 2000

The Communication Cord, Faber and Faber, 1983

Crystal and Fox, Faber and Faber, 1970

The Gold in the Sea (short stories), Gollancz, 1966

Lovers, Faber and Faber, 1969

A Saucer of Larks (short stories), Gollancz, 1962

Selected Plays: 1, Faber and Faber, 1984
  Includes *Philadelphia, Here I Come!, The Freedom of the City, Living Quarters, Aristocrats, Faith Healer, Translations*
Selected Plays: 2, Faber and Faber, 1999
  Includes *Dancing at Lughnasa, Fathers and Sons, Making History, Wonderful Tennessee, Molly Sweeney*

CRITICAL STUDIES OF FRIEL'S PLAYS

Elmer Andrews, *The Art of Brian Friel: Neither Dream nor Reality*, Macmillan, 1995

Sean Connolly, 'Translating History: Brian Friel and the Irish Past' in Alan Peacock, ed., *The Achievement of Brian Friel*, Colin Smythe, 1992
  Connolly points out the historical inaccuracies in *Making History*, and wonders if Friel is playing 'a subtle practical joke at the expense of the hapless academic fact checker'.

Tony Corbett, *Brian Friel: Decoding the Language of the Tribe*, Liffey Press, 2002

Tony Coult, *About Friel: The Playwright and the Work*, Faber and Faber, 2003
  Coult's book provides an overview of Irish history, an account of Friel's life, a description of each play and extracts from interviews with Friel

Ulf Dantanus, *Brian Friel: A Study*, Faber and Faber, 1988

Nesta Jones, *Faber Critical Guide: Brian Friel*, Faber and Faber, 2000

William Kerwin, *Brian Friel – A Casebook*, Garland Publishing, 1997

Christopher Murray, 'Brian Friel's *Making History* and the Problem of Historical Accuracy' in Geert Lernout, ed., *The Crows Behind the Plough: History and Violence in Anglo-Irish Poetry and Drama*, Rodopi, 1991
  Murray is kinder about Friel's distortion of history than Sean Connolly

Alan Peacock, ed., *The Achievement of Brian Friel*, Colin Smythe, 1992
> A collection of essays, which cover a useful range of issues pertinent to an understanding of Friel's plays

Richard Pine, *The Diviner: The Art of Brian Friel*, University College Dublin Press, 1999
> This is the second revised edition of Pine's *Brian Friel and Ireland's Drama*, Routledge, 1990

FRIEL'S SOURCES AND SECONDARY READING

Matthew J. Byrne, trans., *The Irish War of Defence 1598–1600. Extracts from the* De Hibernia Insula Commentarius *of Peter Lombard, Archbishop of Armagh*, Cork University Press, 1930

Pope Clement VIII, *Bull of Indulgence*, in *Calendar of the Carew Manuscripts, Preserved in the Archiespiscopal Library at Lambeth, 1589–1600*, 1869, ed. J. S. Brewer and William Bullen, Longman, 1869

Thomas Kilroy, *The O'Neill*, Gallery Press, 1995
> A play written in 1962 about O'Neill's rebellion, written by a man who later became one of the co-directors of the Field Day board

Lughaidh O'Clery, *The Life of Hugh Roe O'Donnell, Prince of Tirconnell (1586–1602). Now first published from Cucogry O'Clery's Irish Manuscript in the R .I. Academy, with Historical Introduction, Translation, Notes, and Illustrations, by the Rev. Denis Murphy*, Sealy, Bryers and Walker, 1893 (first published 1603)

Sean O'Faolain, *The Great O'Neill: A Biography of Hugh O'Neill, Earl of Tyrone, 1550–1616*, Longman, 1942
> The most important source for *Making History*. O'Faolain was a novelist, and this is a novelistic approach to writing history. Many key scenes of Friel's play are based word for word on O'Faolain's book

Hugh O'Neill, 'The Humble Submission of the Earl of Tyrone Before the Lord Deputy and Council, at Dublin, the 8th of April of 1603', in *Calendar of the State Papers, Relating to Ireland, of the Reign of James I, 1603–1606*, ed. C. W. Russell and J. P. Prendergast, Longman, 1872

IRISH DRAMA

Christopher Fitz-Symon, *Irish Theatre*, Thames and Hudson, 1983

Des Hickey and Gus Smith, *A Paler Shade of Green*, Les Frewin, 1972
> A collection of Irish dramatists' statements concerning their own work, including a chapter by Friel

J. Ellen Gainor, ed., *Imperialism and Theatre: Essays on World Theatre Drama and Performance*, Routledge, 1995

Marilynn J. Richtarik, *Acting Between the Lines: The Field Day Theatre Company and Irish Cultural Politics 1980–1984*, Oxford English Monographs, 1995
> The definitive study of the influence of Field Day on modern Irish politics

James Acheson, ed., *British and Irish Drama Since 1960*, Macmillan, 1993

LITERARY AND HISTORICAL BACKGROUND

S. J. Connolly, ed., *The Oxford Companion to Irish History*, Oxford University Press, 1998
> This book provides a useful overview of key historical events and figures in Ireland's past and present

Seamus Deane, *A Short History of Irish Literature*, Hutchinson, 1986

Arthur Marwick, *The Nature of History*, Macmillan, 1970
> Marwick's book offers a well-written analysis of the nature of the historian's task

T. W. Moody, F. X. Martin, F. J. Byrne, eds., *A New History of Ireland. Volume 3: Early Modern Ireland: 1534–1691*, Clarendon Press, 1976
> This volume of the *New History of Ireland* provides a thorough analysis of the events preceding, during and following O'Neill's rebellion

Hiram Morgan, *Tyrone's Rebellion: The Outbreak of the Nine Years' War in Tudor Ireland*, Boydell Press, 1993
> Morgan's account of O'Neill's rebellion is scathing of Sean O'Faolain's approach to historiography. Morgan is reluctant to relinquish the idea of a single 'truth' of history, and argues for a professionalisation of historical research

John Tosh, *The Pursuit of History*, Longman, 2005
> Tosh's book is an excellent introduction to the question of historical methodology, and is extremely useful for an understanding of the different viewpoints articulated by Lombard and O'Neill in *Making History*. The new 2005 edition covers recent developments in post-modern historiography, which are particularly relevant to an understanding of Lombard's point of view

Robert Welch, ed., *The Oxford Companion to Irish Literature*, Oxford University Press, 1996
> This text addresses key concepts and themes relevant to Irish literature

WEBSITES

www.theflightoftheearls.net

An invaluable source for anyone interested in the history of O'Neill's rebellion, and the subsequent Flight of the Earls to the continent in 1607. The site contains images, historical documents, and descriptions of all the influential figures

www.bbc.co.uk/history

The BBC's history pages contain a timeline, an overview of O'Neill's rebellion, and much information regarding the Renaissance in England and Ireland

anachronism a term to describe the disruption, or falsification, of 'real' time

bathos a descent, often ludicrous and funny, from the elevated to the commonplace

conjunction a word which links words, phrases, or clauses. 'And' and 'or' are both conjunctions

declarative a statement, as opposed to a question or command

deixis a process whereby the context of a word or phrase is indicated. It 'points' away from the word, to its context in time or space. It includes demonstrative pronouns (*this, that*), and personal pronouns (*I, you*). It is derived from a Greek word meaning 'to show'

empiricism derived from a Greek word meaning 'test'. It is the philosophical belief that knowledge originates from experimentation. Empiricism denies the power of individual intuition. It tends to assert the existence of an objective reality, and lies behind many modern theories of science

genre a form or category of literature. Poetry, drama, and fiction are all separate genres. Genres can be broken down into sub-genres. 'Anglo-Irish drama' is a sub-genre of drama

hiatus a gap, pause or interruption

hyperbole a form of exaggeration, or over-statement. It is often unrealistic, for example, 'I'm so hungry I could eat a horse'

interrogative a question

ironic when a word is used to express a meaning opposite to its literal sense, often used for sarcastic humorous effect

metaphor a figure of speech in which comparison is made between apparently unrelated subjects. One subject might be described 'like' another, or it may be described 'as' another

microcosm derived from Greek 'micro', small, and 'cosmos', world. It uses a small system to represent a larger one. For example, many of Friel's plays are set in the fictional village of Baile Beag, which means 'small place'. Baile Beag is used to represent national political events; it is a microcosm of the nation

monologue the speech of a single character on stage, who either addresses the audience directly, or simply thinks aloud, revealing their inner thoughts and feelings

objectivity usually associated with words such as reality and truth, objectivity denotes the belief that an object would exist regardless of whether a person (a 'subject') can perceive it

oxymoron a figure of speech which joins two contradictory meanings

post-colonialism post-colonialism is a term applied to literature written in the aftermath of a history of colonialism. It explores the effect of that history on the colonised country. In literary critical terms, post-colonial criticism reads literature with a particular attention to the relationship between the colonising and colonised nations

primary source a text or document used as evidence, rather than commentary or interpretations, which form secondary sources

realism in literature, realism refers to the representation of everyday characters, in their usual setting, without romanticisation or exaggeration

Renaissance a term, meaning 'rebirth', to describe the historical period that followed the medieval era, and lasted from the 1400s to the 1600s. It was defined by the rebirth of ancient Greek and Latin ideas, which dominated the spheres of art, literature and architecture

rhetoric devices used in persuasive, and artificial, speech. A rhetorical question is a question that doesn't require an answer; its importance resides in its own eloquence, rather than its grammatical or logical function

sign (signifier and signified) these are structuralist terms for the components of a word. The verbal aspect of a word, its letters and sound, is the 'signifier'. The concept it represents, the image it induces when it is written or said, is the 'signified'. The two together comprise the 'sign'

soliloquy a character's conversation with himself. A dramatic convention whereby private thoughts and feelings can be made known to the audience

structuralism in linguistics, structuralism pays attention to the systems underlying language. Structuralism is not interested in spoken language, dialects, accents, and social habits of speech. It explores how words relate to one another in the abstract system of language

subjective the opposite of objective. Whereas objectivity denotes the belief that an object would exist regardless of whether a person (a 'subject') can perceive it, subjectivity believes reality lies in human interpretations

synonym an alternative term possessing exactly the same meaning as an original word or concept

syntax the structure of a sentence, and the way in which different types of words (nouns, verbs, adverbs, prepositions etc) are ordered

Rachel Hewitt is a graduate of Cambridge University and has published essays on William Wordsworth, Daniel Defoe, and topography in literature. She is also interested in the relationship between English and Irish literary and scientific communities.

Maya Angelou
I Know Why the Caged Bird Sings

Jane Austen
Pride and Prejudice

Alan Ayckbourn
Absent Friends

Elizabeth Barrett Browning
Selected Poems

Robert Bolt
A Man for All Seasons

Harold Brighouse
Hobson's Choice

Charlotte Brontë
Jane Eyre

Emily Brontë
Wuthering Heights

Brian Clark
Whose Life is it Anyway?

Robert Cormier
Heroes

Shelagh Delaney
A Taste of Honey

Charles Dickens
David Copperfield
Great Expectations
Hard Times
Oliver Twist
Selected Stories

Roddy Doyle
Paddy Clarke Ha Ha Ha

George Eliot
Silas Marner
The Mill on the Floss

Anne Frank
The Diary of a Young Girl

William Golding
Lord of the Flies

Oliver Goldsmith
She Stoops to Conquer

Willis Hall
The Long and the Short and the Tall

Thomas Hardy
Far from the Madding Crowd
The Mayor of Casterbridge
Tess of the d'Urbervilles
The Withered Arm and other Wessex Tales

L. P. Hartley
The Go-Between

Seamus Heaney
Selected Poems

Susan Hill
I'm the King of the Castle

Barry Hines
A Kestrel for a Knave

Louise Lawrence
Children of the Dust

Harper Lee
To Kill a Mockingbird

Laurie Lee
Cider with Rosie

Arthur Miller
The Crucible
A View from the Bridge

Robert O'Brien
Z for Zachariah

Frank O'Connor
My Oedipus Complex and Other Stories

George Orwell
Animal Farm

J. B. Priestley
An Inspector Calls
When We Are Married

Willy Russell
Educating Rita
Our Day Out

J. D. Salinger
The Catcher in the Rye

William Shakespeare
Henry IV Part I
Henry V
Julius Caesar
Macbeth
The Merchant of Venice
A Midsummer Night's Dream
Much Ado About Nothing
Romeo and Juliet
The Tempest
Twelfth Night

George Bernard Shaw
Pygmalion

Mary Shelley
Frankenstein

R. C. Sherriff
Journey's End

Rukshana Smith
Salt on the snow

John Steinbeck
Of Mice and Men

Robert Louis Stevenson
Dr Jekyll and Mr Hyde

Jonathan Swift
Gulliver's Travels

Robert Swindells
Daz 4 Zoe

Mildred D. Taylor
Roll of Thunder, Hear My Cry

Mark Twain
Huckleberry Finn

James Watson
Talking in Whispers

Edith Wharton
Ethan Frome

William Wordsworth
Selected Poems

A Choice of Poets

Mystery Stories of the Nineteenth Century including The Signalman

Nineteenth Century Short Stories

Poetry of the First World War

Six Women Poets

For the AQA Anthology:

Duffy and Armitage & Pre-1914 Poetry

Heaney and Clarke & Pre-1914 Poetry

Poems from Different Cultures

Margaret Atwood
Cat's Eye
The Handmaid's Tale

Jane Austen
Emma
Mansfield Park
Persuasion
Pride and Prejudice
Sense and Sensibility

William Blake
Songs of Innocence and of Experience

Charlotte Brontë
Jane Eyre
Villette

Emily Brontë
Wuthering Heights

Angela Carter
Nights at the Circus
Wise Children

Geoffrey Chaucer
The Franklin's Prologue and Tale
The Merchant's Prologue and Tale
The Miller's Prologue and Tale
The Prologue to the Canterbury Tales
The Wife of Bath's Prologue and Tale

Samuel Coleridge
Selected Poems

Joseph Conrad
Heart of Darkness

Daniel Defoe
Moll Flanders

Charles Dickens
Bleak House
Great Expectations
Hard Times

Emily Dickinson
Selected Poems

John Donne
Selected Poems

Carol Ann Duffy
Selected Poems

George Eliot
Middlemarch
The Mill on the Floss

T. S. Eliot
Selected Poems
The Waste Land

F. Scott Fitzgerald
The Great Gatsby

E. M. Forster
A Passage to India

Charles Frazier
Cold Mountain

Brian Friel
Making History
Translations

William Golding
The Spire

Thomas Hardy
Jude the Obscure
The Mayor of Casterbridge
The Return of the Native
Selected Poems
Tess of the d'Urbervilles

Seamus Heaney
Selected Poems from 'Opened Ground'

Nathaniel Hawthorne
The Scarlet Letter

Homer
The Iliad
The Odyssey

Aldous Huxley
Brave New World

Kazuo Ishiguro
The Remains of the Day

Ben Jonson
The Alchemist

James Joyce
Dubliners

John Keats
Selected Poems

Philip Larkin
The Whitsun Weddings and Selected Poems

Ian McEwan
Atonement

Christopher Marlowe
Doctor Faustus
Edward II

Arthur Miller
Death of a Salesman

John Milton
Paradise Lost Books I & II

Toni Morrison
Beloved

George Orwell
Nineteen Eighty-Four

Sylvia Plath
Selected Poems

Alexander Pope
Rape of the Lock & Selected Poems

William Shakespeare
Antony and Cleopatra
As You Like It
Hamlet
Henry IV Part I
King Lear
Macbeth
Measure for Measure
The Merchant of Venice
A Midsummer Night's Dream
Much Ado About Nothing
Othello
Richard II
Richard III
Romeo and Juliet
The Taming of the Shrew
The Tempest
Twelfth Night
The Winter's Tale

George Bernard Shaw
Saint Joan

Mary Shelley
Frankenstein

Bram Stoker
Dracula

Jonathan Swift
Gulliver's Travels and A Modest Proposal

Alfred Tennyson
Selected Poems

Alice Walker
The Color Purple

Oscar Wilde
The Importance of Being Earnest

Tennessee Williams
A Streetcar Named Desire
The Glass Menagerie

Jeanette Winterson
Oranges Are Not the Only Fruit

John Webster
The Duchess of Malfi

Virginia Woolf
To the Lighthouse

William Wordsworth
The Prelude and Selected Poems

W. B. Yeats
Selected Poems

Metaphysical Poets